Vietnam Diary

As if on cue, a Viet Cong soldier raised the lid of his position a few inches and slid his rifle barrel forward. A moment ago, there had been nothing there. The top of the hole was perfectly camouflaged with mud and bits of grass. Boyd fired his M-16 from the hip, his shots going far to the left of the target, smacking harmlessly into the mud. Dancer was closer and his shots more accurate, his Thompson hammering its distinctive sound as the big, soft-nosed bullets tore the lid off the spider hole and blew the hidden enemy's head away. The man's body seemed to leap upwards under the impact, spraying torrents of blood in every direction before disappearing back into the hole. Boyd stood transfixed-mesmerized. It was the first enemy he had actually seen, a scant dozen yards away. The Viet Cong were no longer a legend, a myth, a story. They were real and they were here.

Vietnam Diary

by

Steven N. Spetz

Commonwealth
Publications

A Commonwealth Publications Paperback
VIETNAM DIARY

This edition published 1997
by Commonwealth Publications
9764 - 45th Avenue,
Edmonton, AB, CANADA T6E 5C5
All rights reserved
Copyright © 1995 by Steven N. Spetz

ISBN: 1-55197-133-X

Designed by: Dave Buck

Printed in Canada

To the Missing in Action and Prisoners of War

Save a place for men brave and kind,
For those noble heroes left behind,
They honoured the Code,
but did not know,
Who was friend and who was foe.

Chapter 1
THE FIRST DAYS

DAY 358. JANUARY 22, 1967. I have decided to number the days in the "count down" method that is commonly used. Every man knows the day of his DEROS (Date of Effective Rotation Overseas). Men greet each other with the question: "How many days?" rather than the normal "hello." It's like a contest. The man with the smaller number of days regards himself as a superior being. A high number is regarded with expressions of pity and much head shaking.

From the moment the transport plane touched down at Bien Hoa air base, I have been shuffled from place to place, person to person. I feel like the bucket in the "bucket brigade," being passed along without anyone taking the slightest interest in me as a person. Thirty of us spent a week *at Camp Bearcat, the base camp of the 9th Infantry Division, going through an orientation program. They took our American dollars and gave us "script" which looks like "Monopoly" money. We were issued jungle fatigues, jungle boots and M-16 rifles. They taught us about booby traps, tactics and patrolling. Somehow, I have my doubts that any of this will be of use. The old grunts who were teaching the course were only interested in their DEROS and how much they could drink. Everything seems to be expressed in some sort of Morse Code. The enemy is VC or NVA. The government forces are called ARVN. There are RPG's and FAC's. We are FNG, which means Fucking New Guys. I may never be able to speak real words again. Tomorrow I am to be sent to join my unit, Bravo Company, 2-47th Infantry, somewhere in the Mekong Delta. A sergeant told me that some units have lost 80% of their original strength. I don't believe that, but what if it's true? It is incredibly hot here. I haven't really slept since I arrived. The artillery batteries fire all night. How can anyone sleep next to that?*

"Wheredjadobasic?" asked Platoon Sergeant Hardin as he began sorting all of

Boyd's equipment into two piles. Hardin had an annoying manner of speaking without moving his jaw, thrusting the half-intelligible words through tightly pursed lips in a single torrent of sounds.

"Basic?" Boyd asked as he watched Hardin throw his gas mask into a growing heap at the foot of the ramp of the armored personnel carrier.

"Basic training! Whadahell yo' think I'm talking 'bout?"

"Fort Polk. I took basic at Polk."

"Wheresat?" Hardin asked, looking up in obvious disgust at the FNG newly assigned to his platoon, First Platoon. He was holding Boyd's bayonet in his hand as if it was trash. Hardin was a near-giant of a man. The bayonet looked like a toy in his massive fingers. Boyd had an instant image of Sonny Liston in fatigues. Hardin shook his woolly head in dismay, tossing droplets of sweat in every direction.

"Who give yo' all dis shit?" he demanded.

"Polk is in Louisiana. And they issued this equipment at Camp Bearcat."

"Never heard of Polk!" the sergeant replied, accentuating the name as if to suggest Boyd was lying. He stood up, towering a full three inches over Boyd's six-foot stature, and glowered. He looked first at Boyd, then down at the bayonet held tightly in his massive black hand, then suddenly threw the weapon into the "track" with such force it bounced off the far wall with a loud clang before falling to the sandbagged floor.

"And I wish I neverhearda Bearcat!" he added. "Lookadis junk!" Hardin shouted to a soldier sitting on the lowered bench of the track, sipping a can of beer. The man had been watching the proceedings with detached interest. "Gawdamighty, what do those motherhumpers think we do out here?"

Getting no reaction from the man sitting in the track, Hardin turned his attention back to Boyd. The anger vanished almost as suddenly as it had arisen. Hardin's tone became businesslike.

"Awright, Cherry. Forget everything dey told yo' at Polk. Forget what dey told yo' at Bearcat. Forget what yo' great granddaddy who fought in the civil war told yo'. Yo' carry what I tell yo' to carry and nothin' else. Gotit?"

"Yes, sergeant," Boyd mumbled.

"No goddam gas mask. No goddam bayonet. Yo' carry two hundred M-16 rounds. Two frag grenades, one smoke. Three canteens of water. Got three?"

"Two."

"Getja another. Four sandbags. First aid kit. Two days' C-rats. Bug repellent. Gun oil. Salt tablets. Ammo, grenades, one canteen on yo' belt or in yo' pockets. Everything else in the rucksack. We get into shit, drop the ruck. Doan need dat stuff to fight. Find the ruck later. Gottit?"

Boyd nodded.

"We divide up some of the other things. Each man carries his share. Yo' carry an extra radio battery and one belt for the M-60 machine gun. If dey get wet or muddy, I will personally have yo' ass. Take off dem dog tags."

Puzzled, Boyd removed the chain from around his neck, the two metal tags clinking softly against one another. He handed them to the sergeant.

Hardin, muttering something Boyd could not decipher, opened the chain and removed one tag, then snapped the fastener shut. He held the detached tag three inches from Boyd's nose.

"Dis one yo' lace in a boot. The chain goes through the top buttonhole of yo' shirt, then into a pocket. Doan want no metal touching skin here. Rub the skin

clean off. One tag top, one bottom. Gottit?
Step on a mine or get hit by a mortar shell,
we'll probably find one tag to identify yo'
ass. Isatclear?"

Boyd nodded once again.

Hardin leaned forward until his face
was only two inches from Boyd's. The last
time someone had done that was a drill
instructor who had found grit in Boyd's
rifle. He wanted to resist the man's glare,
but squelched the urge. Only dogs and recruits lose staring contests.

"Boyd, maybe yo' think you know
something, but yo' don't. Cherry like yo',
he don't know shit from shoe polish. Yo'
watch, listen, learn. Yo' might stay alive.
Do yo' job, nobody mess wid yo'. Fuck up
and get one of my men killed, Charlie won't
have to waste yo' ass. I'll do it myself. Got
questions 'bout dat?"

"No questions," Boyd said, hoping the
man would have some more pressing
things to do. He only wanted to get out of
the direct rays of the sun.

Hardin relaxed slightly and moved
back, silently surveying the soldier before
him as if he could read his brain waves.

"Awright. Yo' in first squad. Squad
leader is Sergeant Ioneu. Professional.
Knows what he's doin'."

Hardin turned and walked over the ramp of the track and shouted at the man inside.

"Jap! This is Boyd. Get him squared away by 1700 hours. Yo' squad has ambush tonight. Dis Cherry goes wid you. Start learning him-now!"

Hardin jerked his thumb, ordering Boyd inside the track. Then he disappeared, striding purposefully despite the intense heat.

Boyd walked up the ramp, ducked his head and sat down on the narrow bench. The inside of the vehicle was a model of disorder. Equipment was strewn everywhere. The floor was completely covered with filled sandbags. Flak jackets and weapons were hung on hooks. C-ration boxes, a drink cooler and general debris completed the decorum.

He waited for Sergeant Ioneu to pick up where Hardin had left off, but the man just continued taking generous swigs from a can of beer. Ioneu was not exactly displaying the perfect "uniform of the day." He had removed his shirt, boots and socks, and his pants were rolled up to his knees. He was a small, muscular man with definite oriental features partially hidden by oversized, plastic sunglasses. Boyd tried to look at the man without staring, but could not help but notice that the sergeant seemed like a mass of small wounds. Nearly every visible part of his body was collection of red welts, cuts and scabs. The skin of his feet looked like gray prunes, shriveled and ugly. The track reaked of body odor so strong Boyd thought a corpse must be under the sandbags. But he was grateful just to be out of the sun. He was soaked with sweat and his mouth was so dry he could not find enough saliva to make his tongue move properly. Several minutes passed before Ioneu reached into a metal cooler with one broken hinge, took out a beer and tossed it into Boyd's lap. It was warm but it was liquid, and Boyd was thankful for that.

"We sometimes get ice," the sergeant said as he took another can for himself. "But even when it's warm, beer is better than the water with tablets in it. How many days you got?"

"Three hundred, fifty-seven," Boyd answered truthfully, knowing how terrible it sounded. He looked around for something to open the beer can.

"Sheeeiiiitttt!" Ioneu retorted, somehow making a one syllable word into three. "If I had that many days, I'd kill myself right now. Jesus Christ on a pogo stick, that's a lifetime, man. I have ninety-five and a wake-up."

Ioneu threw a flak jacket off the bench, unveiling a hunting knife in a magnificent inlaid leather sheath. He handed it to Boyd.

"Put this on your belt. Bayonet's useless as tits on a hog. A good knife is essential. You can do all kinds of things with it, including opening your beer. But this is the blade a man really needs."

Ioneu turned over his pistol belt and drew his own knife from its sheath. It looked like a small sword.

"Bowie knife," he explained as he deftly punched two holes in the top of the can. His voice sounded somewhat slurred and Boyd wondered if he wasn't a bit drunk. He looked at the knife he had been given. The word "Buck" was stamped on the blade and the letters "W.M." on the handle.

"Whose is it, Sergeant Ioneu?" he asked as he mimicked the squad leader's way of opening the can.

"You can call me 'Jap.' Everyone does. We ain't much on formality or military protocol or that shit. It's yours, now. The man who used to own it won't be needing it. Mac went home in a body bag last week."

"Are you...Japanese-American?" Boyd asked as he drank nearly half the contents of the can in one swallow.

The warm liquid tasted sour and foamy but it was much appreciated.

"Hell, no. I'm Hawaiian. But Hardin stuck the name "Jap" on me and I don't care. Don't mean nothing."

"Is Sergeant Hardin always like that?"

"Old Hard-on? Don't sweat his ass. He's all right. Like he said, don't screw up and he won't give you no shit. The El-tee is okay, too. Lieutenant Brummel got his brown bar through O.C.S. He's no glory hound or nothing. I just hope he stays alive till I get out of here. The guy he replaced was a real asshole. Wouldn't listen to nobody. He blew himself up with a booby trap so obvious a third-grader could have seen it. Then there's Captain 'Are you questioning my orders?' Adams, the company commander. Goddam ring-knocker, you know? West Pointers are the worst. They're fighting their own war, trying to win medals and get promoted, no matter how many men have to get killed to do it. That man is trouble. The company first-sergeant is a cracker, too. Watson kisses the captain's ass so much the man has to sleep on chapstick. Stay away from him, too."

As if he had exhausted his supply of words, Jap lapsed into silence. He leaned his head against the side of the track, quickly finished his beer, then opened another. He did not offer Boyd a refill.

"Can I ask a few things?" Boyd ventured.

"Yeah. Sure. Ask me. What the hell do I know?"

"Where are we? I don't even know where this place is."

"Sheeeiiittt. Who does? You're in Slopeland. 'Nam. That's all you gotta know."

"Does this place have a name?"

"Yeah, it has a name. This is called Rach Kien. It is on the edge of the Rung Sat. What does Rung Sat mean? It means Charlie-owns-it and if you go in there he will tear your balls off. No one challenges him in there. The villagers have pretty well cleared out. Just old women and a few kids still around. There are about ten hamlets all around here. Down the road 'bout two clicks is the Vietnamese Army headquarters. Arvin is a big fucking joke. Half of them are on the other side. We're supposed to pacify this whole area. The first battalion they sent in here was a leg outfit and they literally got their asses shot off. So they sent us, a mech outfit, to increase our firepower. Stupid idea. These tracks can't move in the rice paddies. We have to stay on the roads, which are mined. There's a 105 artillery battery over there. There's a twin-forty/quad-fifty unit over that way. That's about it. We go out and wallow in the mud, Mr. Charles shoots at us from every which direction, everything gets totally out of hand, then Mr. Charles vanishes. We're doing great."

"Are there a lot of booby traps?" Boyd asked. "Like the kind they showed us a Bearcat, with bamboo stakes and all?"

"That's bullshit, man. Luke-the-Gook don't fight with no pointed sticks. Forget that crap. Luke's got automatic weapons, mortars, rockets, machine guns—everything the Chinks and Ruskies make. And mines. The whole goddam stinking country is mined. Jesus, I hate those suckers. Getting shot, that's one thing. I mean, you expect it. You can kinda see it coming. But mines don't kill a man. They just mutilate him."

"Uh, how many guys in the squad?" Boyd asked, noting that so far he had met only one man.

"Seven others. With you, we got nine. That's the best we've been for a while. At one time we were down to five. By the way, whenever you get a chance, take your boots off. Shirt, too. You gotta let your skin air as much as possible. It's nothing but water, mud and water buffalo shit out here. Pretty soon you'll get trench foot if you don't let your feet dry. You sweat under the arms too much, the skin will just peel off. In this humidity, nothing heals. You get a cut today, you'll have the cut the day you leave. And the medics don't give a shit how bad your feet are. They won't tag a man for evacuation unless his feet are missing. Got it? Rashes, insect bites, boils, leech bites-don't mean nothin'."

Jap suddenly flopped down on the canvas-covered bench and laid his head on a folded towel. He was soon fast asleep. It was a wolf-napping technique that Boyd would soon learn. Sleep was acquired in ten and fifteen-minute spurts. A man could never hope for more.

For lack of anything else to do, Boyd cleaned his rifle and thought about stealing a warm beer from Jap's cooler, but decided against it. He did not need to alienate his squad leader. At least not yet.

Within an hour, other members of the
squad began to return to the track. They
had been trading, scrounging and stealing, mostly from the men in the artillery
battery.

The first to arrive was Emile Dancer, a
tall, almost delicate looking, mulatto with
a pencil-thin mustache. He was carrying
a case of San Miguel beer which he had
obtained in exchange for a copious amount
of marijuana. Dancer asked the predict-
able "How many days" and then snorted
loudly at Boyd's answer.

The second to arrive, Bob Kuhn, was a
round-faced, muscular man who announced that he hailed from Mississippi
and did Boyd want to make something out
of it? He then told his own favorite joke
about the difficulties of a white man from
Mississippi with a name that was pronounced "Coon."

The man with the least to say was Tom
Youngblade. He nodded, grunted something and otherwise gave no recognition
of Boyd or anyone else. Boyd would learn
that Youngblade was half Cree Indian, half
English. He was also a Canadian who had
volunteered for duty in Vietnam, a fact

which baffled the other members of the squad.

Private First Class Walter Tomlinson arrived shortly after Youngblade. The men called him "The Pope," not because he was Catholic but because he claimed to be a minister of some strange sect that only he pretended to understand. That a man could be a minister at the age of 19 was hard for Boyd to believe. But, as The Pope explained, in Tennessee you can do anything.

"How many days?" asked Wilson Olive, a cocky black from Chicago. When Boyd answered, "Olive Oyl" slapped his hand against is forehead and performed a little dance. Then he said, quite seriously, "For a hundred dollars, I'll shoot you now."

Private Judd Knowles introduced himself as the 'best goddam machine gunner in the entire goddam U.S. Army or any other goddam army you wish to name.' Specialist Fourth Class Jesus Madiera, a Cuban from Miami, said he would shoot Boyd for seventy-five dollars. Madiera had shaved his head entirely bald. The contrast with his oversize, bushy mustache was nearly comical. He looked like a Mexican bandit. He chewed gum as if he was punishing it.

With the possible exception of Jap, none of the men was past the grand old age of twenty. Yet, to Boyd, they seemed a generation older than himself. The age was in their eyes and deep facial lines.

Only Jap and Olive Oyl were original members of the squad. All the others had been replacements along the line, at one time Cherry like himself. Kuhn had joined the squad a scant month before Boyd.

At 1630 hours, they ate "C-rats" heated over a small gasoline stove. The rations were World War II vintage, garnered from some National Guard warehouse. The little packet of Lucky Strikes had a green circle on the front and a photo of Douglas MacArthur on the back with the inscription, "I shall return."

Somewhere beneath an inch of greasy preservative, Boyd found the disintegrated remnants of beef and potatoes. The men ate in silence as Jap outlined the ambush assignment they had been given. Five men would go out: Jap, Dancer, Youngblade, Kuhn and Boyd.

"According to Military Intelligence-a contradiction of terms I'd say-we got 'bow-cooo' movement out there. Charlie is bringing in supplies to those hamlets every night. He's either going to overrun the

Arvin camp or he's going to have to go at us. I doubt we're the target because the Little People will cut a choagie at the first shot. Anyway, we're going to set up near that hamlet directly south of here. Informants say Chuck is stockpiling rockets and mortar shells to the sky in there.

"Why don't we just bomb the shit out of the place?" Kuhn asked as he worked the slide of his pump shotgun. The man was a walking arsenal. In addition to the shotgun, he had a forty-five in a shoulder holster and a knocked-down version of the M-16. His cheeks were constantly swollen due to his presence of a large amount of chewing tobacco which he spit at frequent intervals.

"Too many civilians. Hearts and minds, son," Jap replied.

"Get a man by the balls and his heart and mind will follow," Kuhn muttered.

The preparations for the ambush were meticulous. The men stripped their pistol belts of all but the most essential items. Jap gave Boyd a handful of plastic sandwich bags and had Boyd put all of his M-16 magazines into the bags.

"A magazine full of mud will play hell with your rifle," Jap explained. "It doesn't take long to get a magazine out of a bag to reload."

Jap showed Boyd how to paint his face and the back of his hands with camouflage paint.

"Mud will do in a pinch," Jap added. "The important thing is not to have a nice shiny face if there is any moonlight. Shows up like a Halloween lantern."

When Boyd reached for his helmet, Jap told him to leave it behind.

"No helmet. Wrap a green T-shirt around your head and tie it back like so. A helmet makes scratchy noises on branches and things. Take one canteen, full to the top. You take a drink, you drink it all or pour it out. No water sloshing around. Now, look, we're five men on ambush. We're not a fucking army. We see a unit too big for us, we let it go by. If we decide to whack some people, we hit them hard then 'Di Di' the hell out of there. We don't hang around to take no pictures. We take a radio but it is turned off. No static or crackling sound. If we decide to cut and run, we turn it on and squeeze the hand set three times. That is a code that means we're coming back through the perimeter and hope to God some asshole doesn't shoot us. One more thing, you fall asleep on me and start snoring, I'll take my Bowie and carve you a second asshole. Clear?"

Boyd grimaced at the prospect of Jap's surgery and nodded. He could hardly imagine himself, or anyone else, falling asleep on a ambush patrol. They had not yet left the safety of their position and he was already as taunt as a guitar string.

At 1930 hours, Jap conducted his final shakedown. The sun would set in one hour, the amount of time he needed to occupy the false position. The sergeant went from man to man, checking equipment down to the smallest detail. Boyd was somewhat taken aback when he saw Dancer's weapon. The soldier had abandoned his M-16 for a 'liberated' World War II model Thompson .45-sub-machine gun. Curiously, Boyd hefted the gun and found it very heavy. Kuhn carried "Sweet Song," his beloved 12-gauge shotgun, and a bandoleer of shells. Youngblade was armed with a M-79 grenade launcher and a bandoleer of special shotgun shells that could be fired directly at human targets with the force of two shotguns. The weapon could blow away small trees and anything else that was unfortunate enough to be in front of it. Kuhn and Youngblade also carried deadly Claymore mines.

Boyd was surprised to see that Jap had abandoned the M-16 for a Chinese AK-

47. Jap quickly explained that the AK-47 never jammed, no matter how much mud got in it. He kept it out of sight when "the brass" came around. They would regard his actions as "disloyal."

When Jap came to check Boyd, he stopped with a suddenness that instantly announced trouble. The sergeant's face turned an apoplectic purple.

"Take that off!" Jap ordered.

"Take what off?"

Boyd felt the sudden grasp of hands on the front of his shirt as the sergeant tore his hand grenade away and held it in a clenched fist.

"Don't you ever do that again!" Jap shouted. "This ain't no John Wayne movie. You do not hang a grenade from your shirt. You will fasten it on your magazine pouch. You will put the strap around the safety handle. When we set up our ambush, you lay the grenade in front of your position, but until then you keep this damned thing secured!"

Boyd took the grenade from Jap's out-stretched hand. He was painfully aware of the angry glares of the other squad members. Kuhn finally offered an explanation.

"Look, Cherry. You carry a grenade on

your shirt like that and it can get caught on something. That pin comes out easier than you thing. Men have been killed doing what you did. You drop a live grenade and you take most of the squad with you."

Satisfied that his men were prepared for their night's work, Jap led the small column to the edge of the village, past sandbagged bunkers and through holes in the concertina wire. The men exchanged crude jokes with other soldiers sitting on the bunkers, keeping a loose watch on the distant hamlets. The Viet Cong seldom bothered them during the day.

Jap struck out at a fast walk that soon had Boyd sweating profusely. Although the sun was already low in the sky, the temperature had clung stubbornly close to the 90 degree mark. The small amount of equipment he carried seemed to take on an exaggerated weight. They maintained their single file formation, Boyd next to last. Dancer, looking un-perturbed by either their mission or the heat, brought up the rear, his Thompson slung across his belly by a strap.

Each soldier kept a thirty-yard space between himself and the next man. The danger of mines, mortar shells or snipers required that they not bunch up and suffer multiple casualties.

As they walked, Boyd was keenly alert to ev-erything around him. The tension in his muscles had not diminished in the least. He was glad he was not first in line. Jap's warnings of mines weighed heavily on him. He imagined the ground beneath him saturated with endless numbers of silent killers, each waiting for the foot pressure that would throw him several feet in the air, separate his limbs from the trunk of his body, then drop the remains in a pulpy heap. Or a little toe-popper could just remove his foot. A Bouncing Betty could leap out of the ground and blow his midsection away. He wondered if the people who make mines ever, ever think about the men who step on them. Or do they just punch in, build mines all day, punch out and go home to their wives and little children and never give it a second thought?

After fifteen minutes, they veered from the dirt road on to a narrow trail that ran between rows of scrawny-looking trees and bushes. The trail felt hard and firm, rising more than a foot above the surrounding wet fields. Occasionally, Jap brought them to a halt by the sudden upward thrust of his arm. Crouching, they peered outward, men facing left and right in alternating pattern. Boyd looked closely at the terrain and was not reassured. The muddy water resembled a brown ocean, extending as far as he could see, interrupted every hundred yards or so by an earthen dike or berm. Random clusters of trees appeared here and there. The fields stunk of a dead, pungent odor like a septic tank. In the distance, he could see a larger collection of trees and the partial outline of some huts, or 'hootches'. Boyd could not imagine trying to cross that open ground. A man would be visible to a hidden enemy hundreds of yards away. Stringy, grass-like plants stuck up above the top of the water and Boyd could only guess that they were rice plants. Thus far, he had not seen a single Vietnamese.

Jap continued to take his men on a start-again, stop-again course that lasted another twenty minutes. Finally, he halted where a large berm crossed the one they were on. Jap told the men to spread out and keep a sharp watch in all directions. The sun was just starting to slide below the horizon.

Boyd was glad to have the rest period but their loose formation was not what he expected. He was puzzled that the Claymore mines were not deployed. Jap moved next to him and spoke in a near-whisper.

"This isn't the ambush spot. You can bet your ass a dozen pair of eyes have been watching us. They'll report exactly where we are. Except we aren't going to stay here. After it's dark, we'll move to the real spot. There's a river a few miles from here and canals run to the hamlets. Charlie prefers to move at night in small boats. We're going to set up along one of the larger canals," the sergeant said, pointing with his hand past a cluster of small thatched hootches.

Boyd did not reply but nodded that he now understood the idea of the false position.

"After we set up, there is no talking," Jap continued. "We set up in an L-formation. Claymores at the ends of the L. You stay right next to me. I have the Starlite scope so I can see what we're dealing with. No one fires until I do. I don't care if a dink is pissing on your head, you don't move. Got that?"

"Yeah," Boyd grunted.

"We give them everything we have for no more than twenty seconds, then cut and run. Youngblade leads us out, you stay right on his ass. That Canuck can see in the dark like a cat. Dancer and I will pull out last, to cover our rear. We go back by a different route. Some of the dinks who have been watching us will be out putting mines and trip wires along the route we took. Never go back the way you came."

Jap slapped Boyd lightly on the arm, then moved quickly away and took up a prone position where he could cover the path.

They watched and waited. Each man squatted motionless, staring at the emptiness beyond. Boyd wondered what the others were thinking. The sun, which had started to go down quickly, seemed to hang on the horizon for hours before it finally disappeared from sight. Dusk replaced the light, then darkness closed in suddenly. Almost as if upon signal, the mosquitoes found them. They hummed and buzzed in delight as they bored through the repellent the soldiers had smeared on their skin. Boyd looked at his hand in the remaining light and there were a dozen intruders in an area no bigger than a cigarette pack.

Darkness enveloped them like a cloud of ink and Boyd found that his eyes adjusted well. For a person accustomed to street lights and neon signs, this was a totally new experience. The sky wasn't really black, it was a dark blue. Boyd had never seen a sky with so many stars, stars that went all the way down to the horizon. The sky seemed like a giant dome over the earth.

The stillness was suddenly smashed by a powerful bang, so loud Boyd's muscles convulsed in an uncontrolled spasm. The sky was momentarily lit by a brilliant flash of reddish orange. His eyes strained to see the hidden enemy while his hands nervously swung his rifle in a wide arc. His breathing rose to a pant.

"Easy, man," he heard Youngblade's whisper. "That's just the 105 battery. They fire 'H and I' most of the night. Harassment and interdiction, the Redlegs call it. It mostly harasses and interdicts our sleep."

Jap kept them in position for another half-hour, then quietly gave the order to move. Boyd tried to maintain the proper distance between himself and Kuhn but could no longer see the man in the dark. He closed up to within ten feet before he could identify the soldier's outline. He didn't understand how Jap could see where he was going at all.

They followed a small trail that led past a cluster of hootches, then swung due south along a very narrow berm between two large rice fields. Away from the trees, Boyd could see more clearly. Their column looked like a file of zombies or ghosts. He was becoming increasingly nervous. It seemed to him they had traveled miles from their firebase and could not possibly get back if they got into a fight.

The final fifty yards took them across a rice paddy. Boyd stepped into what felt and smelled like a combination of cement, oatmeal and shit. The oozing goo clung to his feet and legs, and each step required a tremendous effort to pull free from the gripping sludge. Each time he did, the mud made a noisy, sucking sound. He was terrified of falling, sensing that he would never regain his feet and would drown in the terrible mire. He momentarily recalled stories of soldiers in World War I drowning in shell holes filled with mud. At the time he read those accounts, he could not picture such a scene. Now it was painfully obvious.

When his feet finally touched hard, dry ground, he groped and crawled up the slippery embankment to the top of a berm. He hoped he would not have to repeat the experience again that night, or ever.

The squad waited while Jap and Youngblade scouted the site and decided how the ambush would be laid out. They were on a stretch of high ground, bordered on one side by a large ditch or canal. The berm ran west towards a hamlet and east to a spot where it connected with a wide trail. Trees and tall grass would provide them with the cover they needed.

Jap positioned his men in the L formation he favored. He was at the bend of the L with Boyd; Youngblade was to their left along the edge of the canal.

To their right, Kuhn and Dancer were lying in the grass, twenty feet of space between them. The two Claymore mines were at the ends of the L, the thin detonating wires invisible in the dark. Jap controlled one; Kuhn the other. There was nothing to do but wait.

Boyd had no idea of the time but guessed it was not yet 2300 hours. It was soon obvious to him that the "hunter" has a particular problem: how to keep his mind occupied.

There was absolutely no way to pass the time except to think about something. Think about what? What did the others think about? The enemy? Staying alive?

Hot water and clean sheets? The first thing to do after getting home?

His mind started to run in reverse. He worked backwards through today, his orientation, arrival in Vietnam, basic training. Basic. How he hated the inane methods and constant verbal abuse of the drill instructors. The hype. The irritating system of dividing every action into parts and then doing it by the numbers. Hours of sticking bags of straw with a bayonet and shouting at the top of his lungs. And the first thing his platoon sergeant did was declare the bayonet a useless weapon. He always suspected that the drill instructors knew they were propagandizing the recruits more than training them. They never seemed sincere about anything they said.

He thought about the day he decided to enlist. He could have waited for the draft, taken his chances in the lottery. No, he had done it for revenge. When he was a kid, he used to run away from home. Whenever he was punished for something, he would run away, believing that everyone would be heartbroken by his leaving. He should have grown out of that but he never did. There were endless fights with his mother about his poor school marks, his choice of friends, smoking pot, drinking beer before he was of legal age. He would stay out all night, sometimes for a whole weekend, just to worry her. After high school things did not get better. Whatever she wanted him to do, he did the opposite. When she watched the news and anguished over "all those young kids fighting that terrible war" he knew he would enlist. He would run away again, join the Army, die a hero and be mourned forever. By the time he came to his senses, he was on the bus to Fort Polk.

He thought about Stephanie and wondered what she was doing at that moment. He had run away from her, too. Their relationship had been going to hell anyway. She was accepted at a zillion colleges. He didn't bother to apply. He was always moody, trying to be the rebel-without-a-cause type. She quietly dumped him and he pretended not to care. He told his friends he had dumped her. He had defended his honor and manly image. It was small solace to him now, lying in the grass, mud-soaked, stinking to high heaven, being eaten by mosquitoes while she was probably making it with her new boyfriend. He saw her once before he shipped out. She said he looked good in his uniform and promised to write. He knew she would, once, maybe.

Jap mercifully interrupted his thoughts by nudging him and handing him the Starlite scope. The device resembled a fat telescope and felt very heavy for its small size. Boyd held it to his eye and was amazed by what he saw. It was not a really bright image but everything seemed to be bathed in a peculiar, gray light that gave objects a two-dimensional look. Boyd swung the scope to the right and saw the trail leading to the hamlet. To the left he saw the open water of the canal, the sides lined with trees. Jap pushed his hand further left. Through the gray veil he could see something moving along the water. He squinted to try to focus better.

Something dark was gliding slowly toward them. Radial projections were moving in a steady pattern. Finally, he could make out the details. Two small boats were approaching, propelled by men with paddles and a rear tiller of some sort.

Jap took the lens from Boyd's hand and glued his own eye to it. Boyd's heartbeat accelerated sharply and he nervously fingered his rifle and groped around to reassure himself as to where he had put his grenade. Jap punched his arm and Boyd realized he was breathing so fast he was panting out loud.

Voices. He heard voices. At least it sounded like human voices. It was a peculiar, honking sound, like geese. He had never heard anyone speak Vietnamese. On the highway outside Bearcat, Vietnamese kids sold beer, cola and drugs to soldiers. But they spoke Pidgin English: "Hey! You buy beer? No? You numbah fugging ten, G.I."

There were many voices. Most had a high-pitched, whining tone. It was more like singing than talking. The Vietnamese were speaking loudly. They obviously did not fear being overheard.

Small lights, the kind made by pen-sized flashlights, appeared along the trail, moving steadily towards them. Lights flashed on the boats which were within fifty yards of the shore. The voices became a chatter of unintelligible garbage. Quacking voices. Singing voices. Boyd couldn't imagine those sounds were really words. How many people were there?

A troubling thought entered his mind. Those high-pitched voices must be women's voices. At Bearcat they had been taught that women often acted as bearers for supplies. Other voices sounded like

children. Surely the villagers didn't bring
their children with them. It sounded like
some sort of social outing.

He wanted to take the Starlite from Jap
but dared not move. Jap could see. He
wouldn't spring the ambush against
women and children.

Voices from the shore alternated with
voices from the boats. Someone laughed.
A half-dozen lights bobbed around in nervous anticipation. The boats made small
bumping noises when they struck the
embankment. Boyd could see faint outlines of people moving about. He guessed
there had to be more than fifty people
there. Why didn't every man have a Starlite
scope so he could see what was happening? He remembered Jap saying they
would not attack too large a group. Would
five men attack fifty?

He heard the distinctive, sharp CLICK
of the Claymore detonator. He had seen
the mine demonstrated in basic training.
There was a time delay between the click
of the detonator and the explosion. It was
one-two, buckle my shoe. Jap had made
the decision and that single click shot
through Boyd's nervous system as if he
stuck his finger in a socket.

Adrenaline poured into his blood. A

roaring sound suddenly dominated his inner ears. He impulsively rose up on one knee and held his M-16 at waist level. One-two, buckle my...

The Claymore exploded in a brilliant, orange flash that momentarily illuminated the Viet Cong like a floodlight. Boyd got a millisecond view of dark, distorted outlines, blurred faces, people caught in various positions, passing objects from the boats to the shore. Little people, frozen in time by the flash as if they had just been photographed.

A second orange ball. The concussion of the explosion hit him in the side like a boxer's punch. It obliterated the shouts and screams of people being torn into bits by hundreds of metal balls as the mines spread their destruction like a giant scythe.

The night turned into a crazy-quilt of flashes, crashing sounds, orange streaks of flame licking out from dark tubes. Jap's M-16 was hammering home in short, hard bursts. Boyd was scarcely aware he was firing his own weapon, not really aiming but just pointing it like a wand. It was planned chaos.

The stink of cordite filled his nostrils. Over the roar, he heard the blast of

Youngblade's M-79. A small cannon. Then he was rocked by two grenade explosions at the water's edge. They were so close, bits of hot metal burned past his ear.

Jap pushed him hard.

"Move!" the sergeant shouted, pushing Boyd to the left. He caught a fleeting glimpse of Youngblade's back as the soldier sprinted away from the killing zone. There was still a ragtag staccato of gunfire mixed with hysterical Vietnamese voices. Another grenade exploded, Kuhn's shotgun barked three times in quick succession.

A Viet Cong managed to squeeze off an erratic burst with a AK-47 that sent tracers zinging over their heads. That enemy was silenced by Dancer's Thompson. The gun sounded unlike anything Boyd had ever heard, firing with a heavy, pounding noise like someone hammering on a wooden door.

They ran for a quarter-mile, not in a panic but in a controlled jog. As Jap had said, Youngblade could see in the dark like a cat. Five men had proven that superior firepower and surprise could overwhelm a force many times larger. The ferocity of their attack still dazzled Boyd, and his emotions were in complete turmoil. They had inflicted heavy damage on the enemy with no losses of their own. He felt good about that. Winning is winning. He felt good about himself. He had been in a real battle. It was an emotional high unlike sex, scoring a touchdown, or anything he had ever experienced. He had upheld his part of the battle. He wasn't a Cherry or an FNG. He was a veteran. An instant veteran.

Yet, the enormity of it all threatened to overwhelm him. He had killed someone. He was thankful for the darkness because he did not have to see the results of what they had done. There were no real people, no blood. Just pop-up targets and silhouettes. Just like the Trainfire Range in basic training. It didn't mean anything. And, when the morning sun appeared and they passed through the perimeter, he had nearly convinced himself of that.

DAY 357. 0900. Have not slept in nearly 36 hours. It seems impossible to sleep and I don't know how long I can function like this. Ambush patrol last night, my first combat experience. Everyone says it was a great success and I guess that makes it so. Jap reported that we killed thirty or forty V.C. I wondered how I would feel about kill-

ing someone. I guessed it would be great or terrible. It's neither. It's just a dumb, empty feeling. I was surprised about how loud a battle is. It was deafening, and that really threw me off at first. I have completed one day of my tour. One day at a time, they say.

By late morning, the squad knew something was stirring. The ominous signs were everywhere. Helicopters bearing senior officers from brigade headquarters shuttled in and out of their firebase. The men who planned great battles huddled in small groups, stared at maps in plastic cases and gestured. The artillery battery was hurling hundreds of rounds at an unseen enemy as giant Chinook helicopters brought them more ammunition in pallets slung beneath the choppers bellies. A single spotter plane made large, lazy circles over a wide area. Sometimes Boyd could see the dark wisps of smoke where the shells were landing. Was the enemy that close?

The soldiers waited for the orders that never came. They cleaned weapons, played cards, read magazines and wrote letters home. Music from the Armed Forces station in Saigon blared from small Japanese-made radios.

Boyd felt dirty clear through to his bones. He asked Jap about bathing and received only a muffled laugh in reply.

"Water is for drinking," the sergeant said. "Only the artillery guys seem to get enough to take showers. You dry-shave. You wanna remove some crud, you take a Mech Sauna. I'll show you how. Bring your knife and get in the track."

Boyd suspected some sort of initiation rite but he found himself sitting on the narrow, fold-down bench inside the armored personnel carrier. Imitating his sergeant's movements, Boyd peeled off his uniform as the other members of the squad closed the ramp and hatch. The ramp motor made a gentle whirring sound as it rose smoothly and locked into place, enclosing the two men in a steel oven, illuminated only by the glow of a single red light.

Jap opened a warm beer for each of them and settled back to wait. The temperature inside the vehicle, already over ninety degrees, began to rise.

"You did all right last night," Jap said idly. His words not really sounding like a compliment.

Boyd just grunted.

"But tell me. What became of your grenade?"

Boyd's stomach tightened and a small sense of guilty panic came over him. He had completely forgotten about the grenade. It was probably still lying on the ground where he placed it last night. His instinct was to lie but something cautioned him against it.

"I forgot about it," he admitted.

"I know," Jap laughed. "I counted the explosions. And I didn't see you throw nothing. Sheeeiiiit, man. You're not supposed to issue ammunition to the enemy. First you try to wear it on your shirt, then you give it away. I don't think we'd better issue you no more grenades."

The heat rose another five degrees and Boyd's body glistened with beads of sweat. Still, they waited. By comparison, Jap's body seemed almost dry.

"You had the Starlite scope," Boyd said. "How many people were there?"

"Oh, maybe seventy. I counted six or eight in the boats. The rest from the village. They were unloading long boxes. Probably mortar shells. Why?"

"Were they all men?"

"No."

"Women?"

"Waddya think? Is there a third sex?" came the terse reply.

"Just wondered."

"Well, stop *wondering.* You concentrate on doing your job, staying alive and keeping the men in this squad alive. You start *wondering* about dinks and you'll screw up. You got many, many months to go, Cherry. It don't get no easier than this. I see you wondering too much and I'll have your ass."

"Were there kids there?" Boyd persisted.

"Who knows? They're little people. What does it matter? A dink kid will kill you dead and he'll be very glad he did. The little bastards watch us, report everything we do. They run messages. They plant mines and booby traps. One of our guys stepped on a booby trap so big we couldn't find enough of him to fill a shoe box. We found these little footprints right there in the mud. Footprints so small the kid couldn't have been more than five or six years old. We've killed ten-year-old kids carrying Soviet sniper rifles."

"Yeah, but..."

"But nothing!" Jap cut him off, sitting up with a sudden jerk. "Are you deaf and dumb? Do I have a speech impediment?

I'm telling you, it don't mean nothing. As far as I'm concerned, my life is precious. A dink's life has no value whatsoever. Worthless. Understand? The day a man stops thinking that is the day he gets bagged and tagged. You see a woman or a kid coming towards you and you think you see a weapon, you kill that dink without hesitating. You try to think it over for even a second, you're a dead man. And I don't really give a shit if you get killed but you had better not do something dumb and cost another man his life. They're all good men in this squad and they all want to go home. If the only way to do that is to kill you, because you're a fucking Crusader who wonders about things, then that's the way it will be. Now, shut up and let's clean off some of this filthy country."

Jap tore the cardboard lid from a box of C-rations and placed it on the seat beside him. Then he demonstrated the mech infantry method of bathing, from the inside out.

The sweat had caused the mud and grime to work loose from his skin. Like a barber, he moved the blade of his knife along the surface of his arm, then wiped the mound of brown matter on the cardboard. The strip of skin he had passed over was visibly cleaner.

"Takes awhile but we got time," Jap said as he began a second strip. "It doesn't do anything for the smell but in this country, who would know?"

Boyd took his knife and ran it along the inner side of his forearm. The knife edge soon piled up a paste of mud and sweat. The idea seemed ridiculous but it was good to be free of even a tiny part of the filth that coated his body.

Jap opened two more cans of beer.

"You don't wanna dehydrate while you're doing this," he explained.

The cleansing continued for another ten minutes before Boyd found the first parasite. At first he thought it was a blob of mud, but when he looked closer, it was shiny and fat.

"What's that?" he asked, pointing at the thing on his leg with the point of the knife.

Jap leaned over and studied the blob, then pronounced a simple verdict.

"Leech."

"A what?" Boyd asked, disbelieving.

"Leech. Blood sucker. Lemmee see your back."

Boyd turned and Jap had no difficulty locating several more.

"Well, get them offa me!" Boyd shouted.

"Sheeeiittt, don't mean nothing. Get them all the time."

Jap poured insect repellent on the brown intruders, then lifted each one with the end of his knife. They fell to the sand-bagged floor, twisting and squirming until he crushed them with the edge of the blade.

"Don't tear them off," Jap explained. "Their suckers will stay in your skin and you'll get infections." Jap then sprinkled a white powder on the bites and advised Boyd to check his crotch.

Boyd's body sagged as he sat staring down at the ugly red welt on his leg. The fatigue and adrenaline hangover, topped off by warm beer, made the simple red mark seem like a mortal wound.

"What a hellhole," he mumbled. "Why would anyone want to fight over this place? Who cares who runs this piece of shit, anyway?"

"Must be a secret we haven't been let in on," Jap replied.

When Boyd emerged from the track, the air outside felt almost refreshingly cool. He hated the prospect of putting on his filthy uniform but it would be another week before bundles of new uniforms were flown in by helicopter.

At noon, they ate a hot meal of A-rations. A Chinook helicopter brought the food in insulated sterno cans along with a water trailer slung by straps beneath its belly. Olive Oyl saw it as a bad omen.

"It don't look good, brothers," he said, shaking his head. "Not good at all. They only send us A-rations when the shit's gonna hit the fan. Condemned man's last meal."

Boyd realized that the other squad members took his words very seriously. Olive Oyl had a sixth sense that the other men respected. He was not educated but he could feel things, almost sense them in the wind, the way some people could predict weather. Some men believed Olive Oyl could just look at a man and predict if he would live or die. Today, the soldier seemed very deeply troubled.

One of the medics, Spec-four Falvo, made his "rounds" early in the afternoon. He coated cuts and insect bites with a paste to prevent infection. Madiera had a deep boil in his arm that had grown to the size of a golf ball. The medic made an incision, taped a small plastic tub inside and covered it with gauze.

"That's all I can do," Falvo explained.

"The infection will drain through that tube. If it gets worse, the battalion surgeon will have to incise it."

"Wop," as the soldiers called him, had been kicked out of medical school for stealing drugs. He had been sneaking uppers to help himself stay awake during the thirty six hour periods he was expected to work with doctors, study and write exams. What had started as a small problem quickly got out of hand and he was popping pills like candy when a senior resident reported him. The battalion surgeon was delighted to have a medic who could do more than patch wounds. He had promised to walk through fire to get Falvo re-admitted to med school.

Wop sprinkled a disinfectant powder on the men's heads, which they rubbed into their scalps, then tried to brush off. Most of it clung like pancake batter. He gave each man a large, yellow pill and made certain it was swallowed.

"Malaria pill," he told Boyd, who looked at it suspiciously. "One a week. How many days you got?"

"Too many," Boyd replied, tiring of the questions.

"For fifty dollars, I will give you enough morphine to kill you," the medic said.

"Nice, dreamy way to die. Save yourself a lot of trouble."

"Wop, I think this pill is poison," Kuhn said. "It makes my skin yellow and my piss green."

"Good. Means it's working."

"Wop, look at my feet, willya?" Dancer called out.

"I see 'em. Two. You got two. That's all the army requires."

The medic closed his bag and walked towards third squad.

"You got a great bedside manner, Wop," Jap shouted after him.

At mid-afternoon, there was a false alert. The company commander called his platoon leaders together and ordered the men ready to move out. They dressed, checked weapons and equipment once more, then waited, sweating beneath helmets and flak jackets. An hour later, they were told to stand down once more.

"Well, ain't this fun and games?" Knowles asked in disgust, throwing his helmet into the track.

"It don't look good, brothers," Olive Oyl said, looking at the sky as if expecting a storm. "Somebody's messing with us."

The false alert and tension did not seem to bother Tomlinson. The Pope leaned against the sandbagged wall of his bunker, positioning himself in the shade of a camouflage poncho liner suspended by two sticks to make a canopy, and opened a book. Boyd had seldom seen the soldier do anything but read. He wanted to talk to someone, if for no other reason than to pass the time. He sat down beside The Pope without being invited. If the man didn't appreciate his presence, he could say so.

"What are you reading?" he asked.

"My battle strategy," came the quick answer. "Everything I want to know about war is in this one book."

The Pope turned the front of the book so Boyd could read the title: The Holy Bible.

"Sure," Boyd scoffed, "if your enemy uses swords and spears."

"The weapons don't matter. War is a singular thing. It never changes. In this book, God has shown us the way to destroy evil. He revealed it to Joshua, to David. He will reveal it to you if you ask Him."

"Are you really a minister?" Boyd asked. Tomlinson had a youthful, freckled complexion that made him look like a cherub.

"I am. I knew I wanted to enter the ministry since I was five years old. I have been preaching and witnessing since I was six."

"I mean, is this a real church? It takes years to become a minister. Surely there is an age requirement or something."

"My church is as real as you sitting there," The Pope insisted.

"Well, how can a minister be a soldier? Why aren't you a chaplain, medic or conscientious objector or something. How can you kill someone?"

The Pope put a small red ribbon into the Bible to mark his place and laid it carefully on his rucksack.

"Christians are not pacifists, cowards or wimps. The great heroes of the Bible were warriors. David didn't protest Goliath, he wasted him."

"What about love your enemy, turn the other cheek and all that?"

The Pope's eyes opened wider and he looked at Boyd with an intensity that seemed to burn through him. The man's eyes were such a deep blue that they seemed painted.

"I do love my enemies," he said slowly. "It's God's enemies I cannot abide. This is not just a war. This is the final war, against the anti-Christ."

"How do you know that?" Boyd asked, finding the conversation almost scary.

The Pope opened his Bible once more and spoke quietly.

"I know because God told me."

Boyd abruptly left The Pope to his reading and went to help Knowles clean the 50-caliber machine gun mounted on the track. He had never seen the powerful gun close up. It seemed enormous and the bullets so oversized that he could not imagine being shot by such a weapon and surviving. Knowles was an intensely serious man who genuinely loved the power of guns. He talked about machine guns the way most men talk about sports cars. He showed Boyd how to set the "headspace" on the weapon and described in glowing terms how the gun could cut targets into tiny fragments.

"This is the steadiest gun made," Knowles insisted. "You can zero this sucker on a trail intersection five hundred yards away, wait till an enemy steps on that spot, then...pow! Better than a sniper rifle. Maybe you can fire it soon. I have to zero it in once in a while."

They endured two more false alerts before the sun began to disappear over the horizon. The order came that only one man in three was to sleep that night. And there would be a "mad minute,"a 60 second period during which all the weapons in the firebase would be fired with all the power they had. An enemy trying to creep forward to launch an assault would suffer great losses and be thrown into confusion. It was also a good way to make certain all weapons were working properly.

"Sheeiitt," Jap muttered, after receiving the order from Sergeant Hardin. "We got a bunch of grannies at battalion headquarters, that's what."

"Yo' hope," Hardin replied. "We got bowcoooo movement 'round here. Somethin' going down."

The mad minute had been planned for 0100 hours but the Viet Cong had their own schedule. Shortly after midnight, the first rocket struck the firebase, exploding just behind the artillery battery fire direction center. Some of the red legs saw and heard it coming, like a small comet with a fiery orange tail, arching over the horizon then soaring straight towards them as if it was following an invisible wire stretched across the sky. The Americans had been told that the rockets were crude, unguided, inaccurate weapons. It was small solace to those killed by them. The rockets carried a powerful warhead. They were launched from a simple wooden sled that was just pointed in the direction of the target. Many voices shouted what most men already knew: "Incoming!"

A second powerful explosion just beyond the perimeter sent the squad members into frantic action. They rolled, dove and slid through the entrance holes of their bunkers, piling on top of each other like a rugby scrum. Boyd threw himself through the opening and felt someone land on his back. An elbow or some sharp body part struck him on the head. At first, he thought he was wounded.

There was scarcely room in the bunker for two men but four had opted for the same hole. They were wedged in so tight they could scarcely move but no one volunteered to relocate. They crouched in the body of the hole, avoiding the firing slit in the front. They were not interested in trying to see what was taking place. Not yet.

The explosions began to increase in frequency but the sounds were different. The giant rockets were now joined by smaller mortar shells. The mortars were less deadly but they were accurate and there were far more of them.

A shell landed directly in front of their bunker, exploding with a sharp cracking noise that seemed to pierce the sandbag walls and men's ears. The ground shook as earth, rocks and metal fragments ripped into the sandbags like a hailstorm. The men pressed themselves deeper into the earth. Boyd could not see faces but he heard curses, or bits of words, escaping uncontrollably from men whose voices and thoughts were no longer their own. Amidst the grunting he heard the name "Jesus" muttered repeatedly.

He was jammed down into the small hole that had been dug as a grenade stump, another man's weight leaning heavily against him. A shell exploded behind their position and his lower extremities suddenly felt warm and wet. Blood, he thought. I'm a mass of blood. But there was no pain and it seemed unlikely a shell fragment had penetrated the bunker, passed through another man and struck him. He groaned as his nose told him the truth.

He looked up at the roof of the bunker, a rudimentary combination of cut trees, perforated metal sheets used to build runways and sandbags, and wondered if it could withstand a direct hit. He pictured four corpses in a hole, so dismembered they could no longer be recognized.

As suddenly as it began, the shelling stopped. The other men shook off their paralysis and began to get their act together. Two slid out the rear and disappeared into the darkness. A voice shouted a quick challenge.

"Who's in here?"

Boyd recognized the voice as The Pope's.

"Boyd."

"Just my luck. Get your ass up here. If Charlie's coming in, it's right now!"

Boyd got to his feet and stumbled to the firing port. He looked out and could see nothing but blackness. He had a momentary illusion of dark forms crawling and running towards them, rows and rows of sullen killers over-running them. There was just the black emptiness.

"Your rifle! Where the fuck's your rifle?" The Pope shouted, grabbing Boyd by the shirt collar and shaking him.

"I...dunno."

In his haste to get in the bunker, he had left his weapon lying beside the track.

"Goddamit. Find it and get back in here!" the other soldier ordered, pushing him towards the hole.

Boyd hesitated at the entrance, trying to peer out and make sense of anything. The explosions had stopped and he could now hear other sounds. Overhead a helicopter was making a wide circle, looking for telltale clues of where the Viet Cong were firing the rockets. He heard someone on top of the track pull back the breach on the 50-caliber machine gun.

A voice called for a medic. Not everyone had escaped unscathed. A flare suddenly popped high above their position, its bright glare lighting up the world like a falling star. Still unsure of his legs, he crawled the twenty feet to the track, retrieved his M-16 and pistol belt, then scurried like a weasel back into the hole. He thrust the muzzle of his rifle through the hole and looked over the end at a world illuminated like a carnival ground as more flare shells from the 81-mm mortars popped open and floated towards the earth.

"There's nobody there, idiot," The Pope said in a disgusted tone. "They aren't coming in or they would have been in the wire by now."

Although Boyd wanted to believe the other man, he could not relax his eyes. The artillery battery suddenly began firing, tossing shells at possible enemy mortar positions. It was more a symbolic gesture than effective, for the Viet Cong gunners would have packed up and moved by now. But the shelling required something in return. Convinced there would be no ground attack, The Pope removed his helmet and flak jacket and flopped heavily upon an earth and sandbag bench at the rear of the bunker.

"We'll take two hour shifts," he said in a tired voice. "If you fall asleep on me, I'll slice your balls off." He sounded very serious.

Before Boyd could answer, the stillness was broken by the washboard rhythm of helicopter blades. The machine passed overhead once, then a second time, at a much lower altitude, before it became fixed in one spot somewhere near the center of the firebase. Puzzled, Boyd looked out the entrance to the bunker and could see small lights on the machine which illuminated men running about.

"That's the dustoff," The Pope explained, without looking.

"What's a dustoff?"

"A med-evacuation chopper. Dustoff is the call sign. That means somebody caught it."

"Killed?" Boyd asked.

"No. You don't emergency evac dead men. They can keep till morning. Then, they're the Lord's business, not ours."

The Pope fell asleep with amazing ease, snoring loudly. The shelf was so narrow he slept like an Egyptian mummy, lying on his back, one arm folded tightly across his chest and the other across his face. After two hours, Boyd did not wake the other soldier. He knew he could not sleep; there was no point in denying the other man some rest.

At 0300 hours the shelling and rocketing resumed, but this time it was much further away. Boyd watched with a combination of fear and fascination as the rockets left the tubes with flashes that lit the night sky, then arched across the black dome of darkness until they exploded like an unfolding orange flower. In a different situation, it could be described as beautiful. Hearing no nearby explosions, he went outside and sat on the top of the bunker. In the dim light, he could see other men doing the same thing. He was surprised that he had lost so much timidity so quickly.

The shelling grew in ferocity and was now joined by other sounds. The cracking of small arms and the staccato of machine guns added their peculiar voices to the harsh blasting sounds of the shells. Tracer bullets cut a zig zag, crazy-quilt pattern through the air. Although the Vietnamese camp was three miles away, the sounds of battle made it seem much closer.

"The little people are catching it now."

The voice so startled him, Boyd jumped off the roof of the bunker. The speaker had approached him without making a single sound.

"Fivegetjaten we be up to our asses in alligators tomorrow," Sergeant Hardin said. "Yo' get any sleep?"

"No," Boyd replied honestly.

"Who's supposed to spell yo'?"

"The Pope."

"Well, get his ass up to stand to. Battalion ordered a full alert. We may have to go down dat road. American advisers with Arvin say dey gonna be overrun."

Hardin slipped away towards the next bunker, vanishing as quickly into the dark as he had appeared. Boyd slipped back into the bunker and waited a moment for his eyes to adjust. The Pope was still snoring. After ten minutes, he could see well enough to make out The Pope's form on the shelf. He had not moved an inch. Boyd was also aware of two dots of red light floating a small distance above the soldier's body. He moved closer, leaned down and tried to identify what he was seeing.

Suddenly, with a shrill squeak, the "thing" jumped through the air towards the corner of the bunker. Startled, Boyd fell back and fumbled for the flashlight on his pistol belt. His hand shaking, he managed to aim the beam at the ground. He swung the light in a small circle until he caught the intruder in its glare. A rat, the size of a small cat, glared back at him menacingly, displaying teeth like fangs. The two adversaries remained fixed for half a minute, the man unable to think of what to do, the rodent defiant as long as the light held it in its glare. Slowly, Boyd shifted the flashlight to his left hand and slid his right hand along the belt until he found the knife handle. He felt the heft of the weapon a moment, then drew back his arm slowly. He threw the knife with all his force at the spot where the rat crouched. His aim might have been accurate had his hand not hit the top of the bunker.

The knife missed by a full six inches, bouncing ineffectively off the packed earthen floor. When Boyd swung the light back, the rat had vanished. He had no idea where it could have gone.

"Whaddya doing now?" The Pope grumbled, pushing himself into a half-sitting position.

Boyd didn't answer. He stared at the empty place where he had last seen the intruder. He was sweating profusely and felt terribly weak. He snapped off the flashlight and slid down the sandbag wall to the floor. A terrible throbbing sensation careened around inside his head.

"I can't do this," he said softly, flinging off his helmet and putting his hands to his temples.

"Can't do what?" The Pope asked. "What the hell were you doing just now?"

"A rat. The biggest rat I've ever seen. Actually, I've never seen a rat before. I never thought they grew so big. It was sitting right on top of your chest. Didn't you feel it?"

"No," The Pope said, his voice expressing no concern. "Sheeeiiiitt, man, a rat ain't nothin'. There's zillions of rats. They dig up the old C-ration cans we bury. They practically live in the latrines. Better look down in there before you sit down or they'll bite it off. Rats ain't nothing. It's the snakes I don't like. Big bastards, some of 'em. Not sure why God made snakes."

"I can't do this," Boyd said again. "No one can do this."

"Do what?" The Pope asked as he took the top of his canteen and poured some water on his face.

"Live like this. Like a hunted animal. I'm so damned tired. Filthy. I'm scared shitless half the time. I really am. When that shell almost landed on us, I pissed my pants. Christ, I can't believe I did that. I can't go a year without sleeping. How can anyone sleep with this going on?"

"You get used to it. Everybody's scared. We just hide it. That's the American way. Fearless Fosdick and John Wayne. That's us."

"When men ask me how many days I have left and then say 'kill yourself now and save the bother' I took it as a joke. Now I realize they mean it. I should just shoot myself and get it over with. Vietnam is a death sentence."

The Pope moved across the narrow space between them and dropped down heavily beside Boyd. They could not see each other very clearly in the blackness but Boyd could smell the other man's sweat, decaying flesh and stale breath.

"Look, we all dream of the million-dollar wound. The beautiful, clean would that doesn't permanently damage anything but gets you a ticket out of here. Very few men get it. Most get killed or maimed for life. The rest get the five-cent wound that earns you nothing but pain. Here, put this in your shirt pocket."

Boyd felt something small and hard like a metallic cigarette box being thrust into his hand.

"What is it?"

"A little Bible. It has a steel jacket. Put it in your pocket over your heart. It will protect you."

"I'm not religious," Boyd protested.

"You don't have to be. Just keep it. It will protect you. I promise. Nothing will happen to you."

"But this is yours."

"I have another."

Boyd touched the little book with his fingertips, turning it over and over. It felt cold, hard and lifeless. But he put it into his shirt pocket and carefully buttoned the flap. The weight made his shirt droop forward.

"Everybody is screwed up when they first get over here," The Pope continued. "Just stay close to me or one of the other guys. If I jump left, you jump left. Just stay on my tail like a little duckling until you get a better feel for things. Now, you see, you got me and Jesus taking care of your worthless ass."

Just before dawn, Hardin's prediction began to fall into place. Helicopters carrying excited harbingers of battle planning swirled in and out of the firebase. In the distances, air force planes, F4's, were bombing unseen targets. The planes appeared as minute dots in the sky but the smoke and debris from their bombs was clearly visible.

The company commander huddled with his battalion commander while the sweating crews of the artillery battery pounded out a constant barrage, manning their weapons with a practiced, steady pace. The empty brass casings piling higher and higher behind the guns. The whole firebase began to stink of burnt cordite.

Slowly, inexorably, the poop filtered down. Rumors rose, then vaporized. The facts persisted.

It was no surprise that the Viet Cong had attacked the ARVN camp rather than the American firebase. What was surprising was the size of the enemy force, possibly an entire battalion, and that they were holding the government camp spoiling for a fight rather than fleeing into the vastness from which they had come. The small team of American advisers with the ARVN troop had not been heard from since early morning.

The platoon leaders returned from a briefing with the company commander and brought their squad leaders together. Lieutenant Brummel looked grim-faced as he spelled out what his men would do.

"First and second platoons will be airlifted to an area about five hundred yards north of the camp. Third and fourth platoons and weapons platoon will go by road to a point south of the camp. We will both close until we make contact. Then we try to pinch them until they break one way or the other. We have to force them out into the open."

"Sheeiitt, El-Tee, we're the ones out in the open!" Sergeant Hardin protested. "Where dey gonna put us down, there is no cover atall."

"I already raised that point, sergeant," the young officer cut off the argument. "The tracks and tanks are going down a road that is heavily mined. I don't envy their job, either. Squad leaders, have your people ready in thirty minutes."

The minutes ticked off as men checked
weapons and equipment, set their radio
frequencies and packed the minimum es-
sentials into rucksacks. Long before the
helicopters arrived, the relief column
roared out of the firebase and started towards the beleaguered camp. Two
Sheridan tanks led, their huge tracks
churning up clouds of red dust, long cannon barrels pointed at angles towards the
sides of the road where ambushes might
be lurking. The tracks of third and fourth
platoons followed, the soldiers mounted
on top partially shielded by the armored
cupolas. They wore their flak jackets and
kept their weapons pointed outward. Boyd
squinted his eyes to protect from the dust
as he read the names and pictures on the
sides of the tracks: "The Red Baron,"
"Futhermuckers" and a track with an in-
tricate red, white and blue banner reading "Kill a commie for Christ." A twin-40
'pom-pom' and a squad-50 brought up the
rear. The firepower of the force was impressive, if it could reach its destination.

Minutes after the last of the vehicles
disappeared from sight, the chopping
sound of multiple helicopter blades announced the arrival of airlift. Boyd shielded

his eyes as he watched the single line of "slicks," Huey helicopters that were the workhorse of the Army, make one lazy pass overhead before swooping down in a graceful arch towards the open space in the center of the firebase. The Pope grasped his elbow and motioned it was time to take positions. He felt a tightness in his stomach and a wobbly feeling in his legs. Everything inside him said to run the other direction. Hide. Do anything but get inside those odious, dark machines that now sat on the ground, blades turning slowly, their bodies vibrating gently.

Without an order, which could not have been heard over the noise of the helicopters anyway, the men trotted in single file towards the dark green hulks, bending over to avoid the overhead sweep of the blades. There were no doors on the helicopters and the squads easily scrambled inside past the door gunner who sat impassively behind his machine gun, his face hidden by a plastic helmet and visor that made him look like a big insect. The whole scenario started to resemble a science fiction movie of flying saucers and space creatures.

Boyd squeezed on to a canvas seat between The Pope and Dancer and looked around at the inside of the machine. It seemed stark, almost primitive in appearance, as if it had never really been finished before it left the factory. The metal floor had dark red stains on it. He could guess the origin. Directly ahead of him he could see the helmeted heads of the pilot and co-pilot. The machine smelled of aviation fuel. The Jap shouted something but his words disappeared into the deafening sound of the motor as the blades began to turn faster and faster. Boyd was glad he had not eaten anything that day, for he probably would have thrown up. His hands were sweating so badly that he wiped them several times on his shirt for fear he would loose his grip on his rifle.

With a sudden lurch, the chopper lifted upwards, pointed its nose downward momentarily, then surged forward. The power of the engine was impressive as the bird soared upwards, leaving the earth rapidly behind. Air rushed through the open doors and Boyd grasped the metal tubing of the canvas seat as the machine tipped sharply towards the left side as it left the ground. The speed and thrust of their rise made him gasp. The chopper seemed to leap into the air.

The craft soon settled down into a

steady, throbbing patter as they soared over the fields and scattered tree groves below. The land looked remarkably peaceful and harmless, a blurred mixture of greens and browns in endless squares intersected by berms. Boyd momentarily touched the Bible in his pocket, then pulled his hand away. A drowning man clutching at straws, he thought.

They were airborne for less than fifteen minutes before the "birds" began dropping towards the ground. The door gunner rose up slightly to get a better view and Jap left his seat to squat in the door opening. He, too, wanted a good look at the ground they would have to cross. Boyd glanced momentarily at Youngblade's face. The man appeared passive, almost bored. Surely it was a facade. His nose told him the men were sweating and it smelled strangely pungent. It was not the odor of the gym or locker room after a game. It was the bilious stench of fear.

The choppers dropped very fast, diving down towards the earth, noses headed right for the mud. At the last moment they slowed, as if the pilot had hidden airbrakes, then came to a dead halt, hovering three feet above the rice paddies below. The door gunner gave a sudden wave with his arm, then aimed his machine gun towards the nearest berm. Boyd later learned that pilots never actually touch down on landing zones for fear of tripping mines or booby traps. The Viet Cong sometimes stretched wires across the fields, hoping to catch the runners of the machines. The soldiers would have to jump and pray they did not land on the mines.

Jap led the charge, jumping clear of the machine by several feet, his back hunched over like a fullback. The others were out in seconds, struggling to move away from the choppers as quickly as possible, knee-deep in mud covered with ten inches of water.

Boyd could see streams of men on each side of him, wading and pushing their legs through the goo as best they could, trying to reach the protective cover of the nearest earthen berm. With a graceful hum, the helicopters lifted off, banked to the right and swirled away in the same perfect line formation. The entire unloading time had been less than ten seconds.

Boyd looked back and got a quick glimpse of the door gunner giving them a thumbs-up sign. But he felt he had been abandoned.

They had received no enemy fire but in the distance he could see a gunship strafing an invisible target. The platoon fanned out, struggling against the clutching grasp of the mud, wading until they reached the protection of the first berm. The men fell heavily against the solid earth and laid their weapons over the top towards the ARVN camp some two hundred yards away. Boyd pushed his helmet back and squinted as he watched and waited. It was very quiet. They could see the still outlines of the crude barracks. A Viet Cong flag fluttered from the flag pole. Boyd hoped the enemy had fled. A few yards away, Olive Oyl summarized what they were all thinking.

"It's too quiet, brothers. They're there. Waiting for us."

"Can that shit!" Lieutenant Brummel ordered. "Wilson, where are you?" he called out to his radio operator. "Damnit man, stay close to me. I'm always looking for your ass."

Two Cobra gunships came roaring in from their right flank, popping out streams of 40-mm grenades and hosing down the nearby tree line with machine guns. There was no return fire.

Sergeant Hardin wormed his way

through the mud and flopped down next to the platoon leader. An experienced soldier, he was fit to be tied.

"El-Tee, I dunno who planned dis fucking operation but we are hung out here like a bunch of dumb shits. We gotta move to some cover."

"Cover?" Lieutenant Brummel asked. "Where do you see any cover?"

"Over dere," Hardin replied, pointing to a large clump of trees two hundred yards to their right. "From dere, maybe we can organize something. Out here, we got our dicks up our asses."

The argument was interrupted by the sounds of a rifle as a soldier squeezed off a short burst.

"Anderson! Whadahell yo' shooting at?" Hardin shouted at the man.

"Someone moved in that tree line, sarge," came the response.

"Hold yo' goddam fire! C'mon, El-Tee. Charlie got bow-cooo cover. We got shit."

The officer made up his mind.

"Okay, we'll pound that area, then occupy it."

Brummel grabbed the handset from the radio operator and spoke rapidly to the Forward Air Controller circling above in his single-engined Cessna.

"Smoke!" Brummel shouted. "Pop smoke."

Squad leaders tossed smoke grenades on top of the berm, marking the extremities of their position. The yellow and red columns billowed upwards.

"This is Tamale FAC. Roger, I mark red and yellow," the pilot's voice crackled in the radio.

"Affirmative red and yellow," Brummel replied, his radio ending each transmission with a loud belch of static.

The platoon watched as the small plane made several lazy loops over the target area. The morning sun was just beginning to burn off some of the mist and the temperature, already in the nineties, was starting to climb.

The pilot made a slow, gliding dip towards the stand of trees and unleashed a rocket that hissed downward, trailing a plume of white smoke. It disappeared for a moment into the tree tops, then burst with a small booming sound. More white smoke began swirling skyward. Brummel was content and told the pilot so.

The little plane darted away from the impact area just in time to evade two Phantom jets that appeared out of the mist. They streaked low and fast over the treetops, so close to the soldiers that the men involuntarily hugged the ground. Boyd buried his face in the earth and completely missed the first strike. He heard the roar of the aircraft, the cracking of the air closing behind it and the tremendous blast of the 250-pound bombs smashing into the trees. A tiny moment of quiet followed and he looked up in time to see the second jet making the same run. He steeled himself to watch.

The jet looked enormous, like a flying platform of armaments glued to every part of the fuselage and wings. He could not even guess the speed but the plane passed through his entire area of vision in four seconds. As the jet pulled up its nose, two dark objects separated from the main body and continued on a relentless straight line towards the earth. Any less speed and the plane would have been consumed by its own weapons of destruction. The bombs hit simultaneously. A red-orange flash was quickly smothered by a black hurricane of dirt and smoke. Trees collapsed as if the ground had been dug from under them and bits of wood and dirt rained down on the muddy fields a hundred yards away.

Boyd waited for the order to advance but the jets were not finished. He guessed where to expect them and riveted his eyes on the horizon. The lead plane was back within thirty seconds, approaching at a steeper angle. The front of the jet suddenly began to flash like a thousand Fourth of July sparklers as the 20-millimeter Gatling guns unleashed a torrent of heavy shells that shredded the target area. The wingman added his fire to the destruction. To Boyd's ears, it sounded like a concert of bass drums in a thunder storm.

As suddenly as they appeared, the jets were gone. Brummel gave the handset back to his radio operator and gave Sergeant Hardin the order he wanted: "Fire and maneuver."

Hardin led the first and second squads as they rushed towards the next berm. The other two squads laid down a covering fire to suppress any Viet Cong that might be waiting in the trees. There was only silence.

Hardin's group took what protection they could behind the berm and began firing. Brummel ordered his two squads to move.

Boyd tried to run but it was not really possible. After a few yards, he found that he could do little more than a labored walk, pulling each foot out of the mire with tremendous effort before thrusting it down into the mud once more. He was sweating, trying to move, but felt he was standing still. He bent over as much as he could as if he could make himself smaller. He felt naked, vulnerable, and the tree line didn't seem to get any closer. He pictured thousand of gun barrels hidden in front of him, all pointing at his chest. Every Viet Cong, every North Vietnamese soldier, was pointing his barrel just at him. He stayed slightly back, following The Pope "like a duckling." He felt the Bible bounce in his pocket and muttered, "Do your thing, Jesus."

After an eternity, they reached the berm where the other squads lay prone, firing slower now at the trees ahead. To his dismay, they did not stop. They were going to leapfrog the other squads. They would enter the tree line first.

Fifty yards to go and his legs felt like pieces of cement. He was having trouble breathing. He wasn't running, he wasn't even walking. He was plodding, lunging forward with every exhausted step. He saw Knowles go down hard into the mud, twisting his body at the last minute to avoid plunging the M-60 into the muck. There were no shots, the man had simply fallen.

Madiera stopped to help him up. Boyd gained two steps on them when he saw Madiera suddenly flip over Knowles, both of them thrashing in the mud. Out of the corner of his eye, he had seen the bullet impact into Madiera's shoulder blade. He was stunned because he realized the bullet had hit the man in the back.

He whirled around in time to see a tiny bit of movement along the base of the berm they had just crossed, fifty yards to their right. Now other weapons opened up on them, seemingly from all directions.

"They're behind us!" he shouted as loudly as he could. "Spiderholes!"

As if on cue, a Viet Cong soldier raised the lid of his position a few inches and slid his rifle barrel forward. A moment ago, there had been nothing there. The top of the hole was perfectly camouflaged with mud and bits of grass. Boyd fired his M-16 from the hip, his shots going far to the left of the target, smacking harmlessly into the mud. Dancer was closer and his shots more accurate, his Thompson hammering its distinctive sound as the big, soft-nosed bullets tore the lid off the spider hole and blew the hidden enemy's head away. The man's body seemed to leap upwards under the impact, spraying torrents of blood in every direction before disappearing back into the hole. Boyd stood transfixed-mesmerized. It was the first enemy he had actually seen, a scant dozen yards away. The Viet Cong were no longer a legend, a myth, a story. They were real and they were here.

His spell was quickly ended by the snap of a bullet whipping past his cheek. Fatigue disappeared in a torrent of adrenaline. He ran as he had never run before.

The tree line, which had seemed so elusive, now raced towards him. A moment ago, it had represented danger. Now it was a sanctuary. He saw the first men disappear into the dark greenery and throw themselves on the ground. If there were mines and booby traps, they would have to take their chances. Boyd saw Knowles half-carrying, half-dragging Madiera towards the trees. They were going nowhere, bogged down like two bags of wet sand. No man, no matter how strong, could carry a machine gun and another soldier.

Boyd shifted his rifle to his left hand, grasped Madiera under the left arm ignoring the soldier's cry of pain, and charged on, propelling the trio forward as if they were one unit. He threw Madiera over the edge of a bomb crater, then drove headlong after him. Knowles slid down the side of the same hole, dragging the M-60 by the barrel. He had lost his helmet and was covered with mud. His eyes displayed a wide-open fright.

Everywhere voices were shouting confused and garbled warnings over the hurricane of automatic weapons. The squads were scattered about, crouched in bomb craters from behind burned, broken trees and logs. Eyes anxiously searched for the hidden enemy. Boyd could see three green mounds lying in the field, motionless. Two were face down, the third lying on his back, arms stretched outward. A vile taste suddenly filled his mouth. He tried to spit it out but his mouth was totally dry. If the men in the field weren't dead, they would suffocate in the mud. Nor were the Viet Cong gunners giving any quarter. Boyd could see bullets smacking in the mud around the bodies, making tiny whirlpools where they struck.

"Wilson!" he heard Lieutenant Brummel shout. "Where's my goddam radio?"

Someone called for a medic and he heard the Wop's angry retort that he would get there when he could. Madiera groaned and Boyd looked at the man's face, twisted in pain. The front of his shirt was ripped away as if a giant claw had torn at the man. Blood was pumping steadily through a massive hole marked by splintered ribs.

"Medic!" he shouted in the direction where he had heard Wop's voice. His own voice sounded cracked and so high-pitched he didn't recognize it.

"Sit on it!" Wop shouted back from another bomb crater. "I got two fucking hands and three wounded men here!"

"Wilson!" Brummel continued to shout. "Where's Wilson?"

"He's down!" someone shouted back. "He's out there."

Boyd looked again at the three men lying in the rice paddy. He could see that one of them had a PRC-10 radio on his back, half-buried in the mud. He saw something else. Wilson was crawling through the mud, dragging himself towards them. He was forty yards from the tree line and didn't have a hope in hell of reaching it. Columns of muddy water leaped up around him. Whoever was trying to finish off the soldier wasn't a good marksman but given enough time he would certainly get lucky.

Boyd's eyes fastened on the radio. Without it, they had no link to the other units or the air force. The radio was their life-line and Wilson was trying to bring it to them.

He measured the distance with his eyes and tried to translate the space into time. A minute? Maybe less. He was vaguely aware of Knowles crawling out of the hole, worming his way towards the edge of the tree line, pushing the machine gun in front of him. Like a man preparing for a swim, Boyd peeled off his rucksack and belt, then threw his helmet beside them. Madiera made a noise, opened his eyes momentarily, seeing nothing. He was completely drenched in blood, more blood than Boyd have ever seen in his life. Strangely, he felt nothing. Not horror. Not sympathy.

He placed his hands on the ground and raised his butt up as if he was starting a hundred yard dash. If anyone saw him, they didn't call out.

Hands and feet pushed against the ground as he launched himself with all the speed and momentum he could muster. He dashed past Knowles into the open, his driving legs carrying him nearly half the distance to the fallen man before the clutching grip of the mud finally took hold and pulled him down. He fell forward, hitting the watery slop like a stone skipping across a lake, sliding the full length of his body before stopping.

Mud partially blinded him but he could see Wilson raise his head and look at him, imploring. Boyd didn't try to stand up, he just sprang forward again, splashing in the mud like a frog. Again, pushing with hands and feet, he flung himself another few feet, presenting as poor a target as possible. He could hear the growing thunder of weapons as the platoon tried to get their act together. The M-60 was right behind him and he hoped Knowles would not shoot him in the back.

Another lunge brought him alongside the wounded man who now lay on his side, hands outstretched as to receive a gift. Boyd rose into a crouch position and took hold of one arm. The man seemed attached to the mud.

"Get up!" he shouted as he tried to pull the soldier free.

"Can't," Wilson pleaded, his voice weak and racked with pain. The man's fingers suddenly dug into Boyd's arm so hard it felt like spikes being driven into his flesh. The soldier was a drowning man, holding on to life.

"Get up, you bastard. I can't carry you!"

"No. Shot in the legs."

The sound of weapons firing seemed to double and double again as the platoon fired at every conceivable hiding place where the Viet Cong gunners were becoming equally aggressive. Two men, flopping around in the mud and filth. Both sides knew why. For the moment, there was no other battle. They were the whole war.

Boyd grabbed the radio straps and tried to free the man from the precious device strapped to his back. He abandoned the idea immediately. Everything was hopelessly twisted and pulled taunt. A voice in his head told him to leave the man and run. It was a hopeless mission.

A bullet seared past his temple so close he felt the heat of it. He had an image of his body in the mire, eyes blinking up at himself. We're both dead, he thought, but strangely didn't care. He wouldn't quit.

He crawled on top of Wilson's body, grasped him under the armpits and tugged. The man felt like he was attached to the ground. He heaved with all his strength and miraculously they moved. Struggling to keep his balance, he took small sideways steps, pulling the dead weight less than a foot at a time. What time had he guessed? A minute? Wrong. Hours.

Voices shouting. Everyone shouting words that blurred into a babble of nonsense. He caught a glimpse of Knowles, out of the tree line now, kneeling in the mud, a look of hatred on his face, the M-60 held waist high, firing at something to their right. Lieutenant Brummels's voice screamed orders no one seemed to heed. Boyd heard him say, "Leave him! Bring the radio."

He fell, struggled back to his knees, dragged Wilson another foot, fell again. A bullet smacked into the mud near his face. He heard several more go over his head. Both men were so mud-covered he could no longer get a grip on Wilson's arms. He grasped the straps of the radio and pulled again. Louder voices, then other hands grabbing them both. He got up and stumbled towards the protection of the trees, Youngblade's supporting arm under his shoulder. He fell heavily to the ground, his face pressed against the hard earth, limbs spread-eagle. His chest pained him terribly and he had no sensation in his right arm.

Someone rolled him over and heard Jap's voice ask, "Is he hit?"

Another distant voice. Dancer?

"Doesn't look like it."

A tidal wave of relief. Too drained to move. Voices, so many voices. Lieutenant Brummel screaming on the radio trying to contact the air force. Someone was talking on the platoon's frequency.

"Get off my 'push', you asshole!" the officer shouted.

The company commander's voice demanded situation reports Sitreps. Everyone talking at once. The radio constantly crackled with short, broken phrases as the scattered units tried to restore order: "Pinned down...dustoff...we got wounded here...where's the goddam air support?"

Jap poured some water over his face.

"C'mon, Boyd. You don't get no R and R."

His M-16 was thrust into his hands. He saw Wop working frantically on Madiera, talking to Hardin as he tried to staunch a flow of blood pumping like an open fire hydrant.

"We need a dustoff. Don't you understand that?" the medic asked.

"Where dey gonna land?" Hardin shot back.

Brummel finally got something going. The artillery battery fired a Willie Peter-white phosphorous-shell that exploded two hundred feet in the air. A marking round. Brummel gives directions and the high explosive shells begin to walk in on the enemy.

Brummel and Hardin agreed that most of the V.C. were dug in along the base of a berm running horizontal to the field. Their spider holes were about thirty feet apart. There were more in the tree line by the army camp. Snipers were in the trees and on the roofs of the buildings. The enemy was not interested in a guerrilla hit and run shoot out. The V.C. have opted for a set-piece battle.

Brummel patiently brought ever-increasing firepower to bear on the entrenched enemy. He adjusted the artillery on to the earthen berms, mixing phosphorous shells with the high explosive. Flipping frequencies on the radio, he was able to direct Cobra gunships against the nearest buildings where the Viet Cong had positioned automatic weapons. The huts collapsed like cardboard when the gunships unleashed their rockets against them.

The platoon searched for depressions in the ground and submerged themselves as deeply in the earth as possible. They emptied their weapons, reloaded and emptied them again.

Wop slid into the crater, dropped his

helmet at Boyd's feet and quickly checked Madiera's vital signs. He injected morphine into the soldier's shoulder, then cut away part of his shirt. Boyd took a quick look at the wound, then turned away, afraid he would be sick.

"Don't sit on your butt, give me a hand," the medic demanded. "Let's get him up in the sitting position. Use your knife and cut all of his shirt away."

Boyd's knife blade sliced easily through the cloth. Pieces of green gave way to a mass of crimson. The hole in Madiers's upper chest was the size of a man's fist.

"Bullet hit bone," Wop mumbled, talking to himself, the words coming in short, breathless bursts as he pressed a foil-covered compress of the hole. "That's why it blew out like that. Ain't as bad as it looks."

"Is he...?"

"He'll be okay," the medic said as he wound a roll of gauze around the man's chest. "Seen a lot worse. Seen men with half a dozen holes like that make it. Just gotta get him outta this hell hole."

Next, they pulled Wilson's body to the lip of the crater, keeping his legs extended. When Wop cut away part of the pant leg, Boyd could see that little remained of the man's right knee. The lower extremity of the leg was connected by little more than skin and a few strands of muscle.

"Am I going to lose my leg?" the radio operator asked feebly. The medic shoved morphine into the thigh muscle and promised the man he would be a track star.

"I lied," he said quietly to Boyd as he tried to make a brace to hold the leg together.

The hole was getting crowded and Boyd was looking about for a new position. His squad leader solved the problem for him.

"We're moving out!" Jap shouted. "The rest of the company is pushing in from the other side. It's pay back time, girls. Get your asses out of those holes!"

Inertia and self-preservation had seized the day and the platoon sergeants had great trouble getting the men out of their safe holes. Hardin was everywhere, kicking and cursing men. They were so covered with gray-brown mud they looked like dead men rising from a graveyard. The Viet Cong had stopped firing but no one was reassured by that. Charlie would try to "grab on to their bellies" and fight in so tight the American air power could not be used.

In two's and three's the platoon worked its way along the edge of a small path that led towards the ARVN camp. The ground was blackened, churned up by bombs and rockets. For the first hundred yards, they saw and heard nothing.

In the distance, they could hear the heavy weapons of the tanks and tracks pouring a drum fire of shells into the camp. The armored vehicles were the anvil; the foot soldiers were the hammer.

Boyd became part of a pickup team with Knowles and The Pope. Ahead he could see Youngblade and Dancer working like dancing partners, twisting and turning as they moved, checking front, rear and above. The land form narrowed into a small peninsula, acting as a funnel until they were strung out in clusters behind Brummel and Hardin.

Fifty yards from the edge of the camp, an unseen hand triggered the Claymore mine that blew Lieutenant Brummel away. The mine had been positioned in the crotch of a small tree, covered with small branches. One minute Boyd could see his platoon leader crouched at the edge of the trail, surveying the ground ahead of him. The next moment there was a bright light, like a giant camera flashbulb, a sharp bang and Brummel disappeared into the brush at the side of the path. Hardin barely escaped death as the contents of the deadly mined passed over his head.

The men hugged the ground, weapons ready, looking for any sign of movement, frightened eyes wide open, frantically searching everything around them.

Hardin rolled on his left side and made a hand signal to the two men immediately behind them. He indicated an encircling movement.

Youngblade and Dancer crawled through the brush to a point directly behind where the mine had been hidden. Dancer rose up until he was on one knee, his Thompson ready, head and eyes moving left and right. Youngblade found the wire, still tied to the tree trunk with a blade of grass. His long artistic fingers touched it softly, then began to follow it along the ground. The two men crawled slowly towards the camp, Youngblade holding the M-79 in his left hand, parallel to the wire.

The wire vanished into the ground. Youngblade signaled to Dancer to stop while he slowly drew his knife from its sheath. Gently, slowly, he probed the ground, pushing the knife in several inches, withdrawing it, then doing it again a few inches away. It struck something hard.

Youngblade pried with the blade and the earth rose up a fraction of an inch. He raised his left hand very slowly like an orchestra director about to start a concert. Dancers's eyes never wavered from those outstretched fingers. Boyd watched the two men with a combination of fascination and confusion. What were they doing?

Youngblade dropped his left hand to the handle of the knife, then used both his powerful arms to apply force to the blade. Like a manhole cover, the lid of a magnificently camouflaged spider hole flew into the air, scattering dirt and clumps of grass with it. Youngblade flung himself to the left as Dancer sprang to the edge of the hole. The muzzle of his Thompson nearly smashing into the barrel of an AK-47 coming up out of the hole. The heavy Thompson spurted flame and smoke as Dancer swung it back and forth over the hole like a man trying to put out a fire. As suddenly as he had jumped forward, Dancer rolled to the left while Youngblade dropped a hand grenade over the edge. He had let three of the five seconds tick off before releasing the safety spring. It no sooner left his hand then it exploded with a muffled thump deep in the earth. Whoever was in the hole had no opportunity to try to throw the grenade back.

Amazingly, the guerrilla had enough life left to rise up in the hole, weapon still in his hand. Boyd got a quick glimpse of what looked like a thin, black scarecrow holding a gun. The man never fired a shot and was probably already dead before Youngblade's M-79 hit him, nearly cutting him in two.

The fighting from the other side of the camp grew louder, spurring Hardin into action. The platoon moved towards the nearest building. A sniper shot a man in second squad through the head. Knowles used half a belt of ammunition to flush him out, tearing away pieces of a building with the M-60. The sniper tried to flee and almost ran into the muzzle of Kuhn's shotgun. The blast knocked the man back into the rubble of the building.

The platoon began to fan out, taking what cover they could find in the debris of collapsed buildings, ever mindful of the many hiding places rubble provides. The Viet Cong were fighting valiantly but were being pushed back into an every-shrinking ring near the camp's small parade ground. Boyd could hear the clanking and grinding of tank treads amidst the constant rumble of machine gun fire. The Viet Cong assaulted the tracks with rifle grenades and RPG2 rockets. Most were killed within seconds of exposing themselves but they were inflicting casualties upon the attackers. Two Americans were blown from the top of their track by a grenade. A machine gunner on another track was wounded by rifle fire. Another man took his place and was killed almost immediately despite the protection of the cupola. A third soldier took his place and had most of one hand shot away.

Each yard the guerrillas yielded increased their desperation. They were now forced into an area no bigger than half a football field. Their officers long dead, the flames from the burning buildings threatening to fry them, the remaining Viet Cong decided upon a desperate dash across the open spaces. Boyd saw fleeting glimpses of running forms dashing from building to building. The enemy soldiers were so small, at first Boyd thought they were children.

It was a plan with no hope of success. Hardin shouted at his men in a booming voice as they rushed to the place where the camp ended and the muddy fields began. The Viet Cong were running across the rice fields, ducking temporarily behind the berms for protection, firing wild and ineffective bursts at their pursuers. It was no sanctuary from the helicopters that now had a clear view of them. The platoon was burning up ammunition at a tremendous rate. The men were motivated by a combination of rage and astonishment at suddenly having so many targets at once. The Viet Cong who tried to hide behind the berms were dog meat for the Cobras that criss-crossed the fields like giant black crows on a feeding frenzy. The stink of spent ammunition filled Boyd's nostrils and smoke burned his eyes but he emptied three more magazines into the fleeing enemy.

No one ordered the battle to end. It just ground to a halt. There was nothing left to shoot at. Boyd rose up on one knee and looked across the open expanse. More than fifty dark mounds dotted the muddy fields, like randomly placed stepping stones.

"Boyd, watch your ass," Jap cautioned. "There may be some of them still hiding in this mess."

For the next two hours, the Americans searched the camp for any hidden enemy. Others slogged through the fields and

picked up weapons. Three wounded guerrillas were dragged back to the camp, their
faces fixed with fear of what would happen to them. Boyd stared at them, feeling
a small sense of wonder about this elusive enemy. Others did the same, for they
seldom saw any live guerrillas. They were
so physically small, it seemed impossible
that they could be so dangerous. They sat
close together, hands on the top of their
heads. They seemed incredibly dirty, even
more than the Americans were after hours
in the mire. None had boots or sandals. A
dozen Japanese cameras took photographs until Hardin ordered the men to
end their gawking.

"Goddamit, dey ain't movie stars!" the
sergeant roared as he waded into the curious crowd. "Squad leaders-get yo' men
moving!"

They overturned collapsed pieces of
metal roofing, probed around for spider
holes, and counted bodies. They routed
two more guerrillas out of their hiding
places. They appeared bewildered.

One maintained a permanent, absurd
grin on his face, his upper lip pulled back
tight, exposing a mouth with no more than
six teeth. He looked ninety. The other prisoner looked like a ten-year-old but his

expression was one of pure hatred.

"Watch the little one," Jap cautioned his men. "He is hard-ass V.C. all the way."

There were bodies everywhere, and not just Viet Cong. The bodies of ARVN soldiers, their distinctive "tiger" camouflage uniforms a sharp contrast to the Viet Cong black pajamas, were scattered throughout the camp. All the bodies had been stripped of their boots and personal effects. Most appeared to have died fighting but others had been shot through the back of the head. Their bodies were arranged in neat rows. The corpses were bloated and turning black in the sun. The stench was becoming a serious problem.

Some had been mutilated. Directly in front of the now destroyed camp headquarters, they found an example of how the V.C. heap abuse on their enemies. They had hacked the heads off four ARVN soldiers, cut away the victims' testicles, shoved them into gaping mouths, then impaled the heads upon short, wooden stakes. The grisly sentinels were placed in a circle, staring at each other with permanently open eyes. In the center of the ring was a piece of cloth with some writing painted on it. The Americans guessed it was some sort of propaganda message.

Captain Adams kicked the display over and ordered two men to bury the heads. He had been shot in the right arm but gave no indication of relinquishing command. He ordered the men to bring all their dead and wounded to the center of the camp for evacuation. First Sergeant Watson was one of the dead. As the number of dead and wounded grew, Boyd realized how severely the company had been mauled.

They carried in Lieutenant Brummel's body on a makeshift stretcher, then quickly zipped it into a body bag. No one wanted to look at a headless corpse and no one wanted to look for his head.

The camp smelled of death. They had no way of putting out the fires started by the air strikes, so the buildings just continued to burn and fill the air with black, acrid smoke. The fires added to the heat and the men panted and coughed as they carried the wounded.

Wop and another medic worked as fast as they could, trying to save everyone. It could not be. A man with his guts hanging out and most of one leg missing died a screaming, open-mouthed death as his buddies held his hands down to stop the man from clawing at his intestines. They asked Wop to give the man more morphine but the medic refused. He was running low and there were many more men to be treated. Finally, the wounded soldier gave out a solitary, haunting cry like a tormented animal and died. They let go of his hands and placed a poncho liner over him.

"His mother wouldn't let him play football because he might get hurt," one of them said to Boyd, as if for some reason he thought Boyd should know.

A few yards away Wop was trying to help a man who had a sucking chest wound. The medic's efforts were made more difficult by the man's constant spitting of blood into Wop's face. The medic's shirt was soaked in blood. Suddenly, the soldier's head slumped backwards and his eyes rolled back in his head. Wop sat back on his haunches a moment, staring down at the man's face which seemed strangely peaceful.

"Shock," he said softly. "It wasn't the wound. Shock."

A fierce argument broke out between Hardin and Captain Adams.

"Goddamit, captain, where's the dustoff?"

"Do I know? I've called for it. There's a battle south of here. They can't be everywhere at once."

Wop rose to his feet to join the fray. Everyone's tempers were flaring.

"These men can't hold out forever. I can't keep them alive with this!" Wop shouted, waving his near-empty medical kit.

"Just do what you can!" Adams replied, then stormed off to try again to reach the evacuation ships, leaving the medics to perform medical miracles with bandages.

Between two demolished barracks, Youngblade made an electrifying discovery. Staked spread-eagle to the ground by pieces of wire was a wounded American soldier. He was not a member of their platoon and they quickly surmised that he was one of the American advisors who had been in the camp. The rest were no where to be found.

The soldier had been stabbed repeatedly in the arms and legs. His ears, nose and penis had been cut off. His face was swollen and disfigured by a severe beating. His skin was burned by the sun, lips dried and cracked. Yet he had the strength to warn Youngblade not to approach.

"Don't move me. They booby-trapped me."

Youngblade sought out Sergeant

Hardin who came running. He ordered the men to move fifty feet away, then walked up and squatted beside the prone figure. He poured water on the soldier's face and dripped a small amount into his mouth. Thirty seconds passed, then he gave him some more water. Hardin leaned over so the man could whisper and be heard.

"What can yo' tell me?" Hardin asked.

"Booby traps. At least two. They're underneath me. If you try to move me, you'll blow both of us up."

"We'll find a way," Hardin replied.

"You can't," the soldier insisted. "Maybe you could dismantle one but not both. The slightest movement..."

Hardin sat quietly, giving the man warm water from his canteen.

"What's yo' name?" he asked.

"Riley. Mike Riley."

"What yo' want us to do, Mike?"

"I don't want to get blown up. Shoot me first."

"Anything else?"

"I'd like to confess. I'm Catholic. They never broke me. They wanted me to beg, you know? I never did. Tell them I never begged. Tell them."

"I'll tell them, Mike," Hardin replied, not knowing whom he was to tell. "If it matters, we wasted the bastards. Every one of them."

"They never broke me," the soldier repeated. "Fuckin-A."

"Fuckin-A, Mike."

"I'm afraid of dying without a priest. You know?"

"Maybe we can help you," Hardin said, then stood and walked slowly to where the other squad members were waiting. When Hardin told them the facts, they fell sullen and silent. Lips mouthed curses but no words came forth.

"He wants a priest," Hardin said to The Pope. "Yo' a man of the cloth."

"I'm not a priest," The Pope protested. "My church doesn't even believe in last rites."

"What goddam difference does it make?" Kuhn asked angrily.

"Fake it, man," Jap added. "It means a lot."

"You don't understand," The Pope insisted, but his resolve caved in and he agreed to give the man what religious comfort he could.

The Pope handed his rifle to Boyd and walked, with a dragging step, to the soldier's side. He knelt down, placed his face close to Mike's cheek and began talking to him. The others could hear the sounds but could not discern the words. The man's eyes were half-open and he nodded from time to time. Once he spoke. Two minutes passed, then three. The Pope spoke in a constant monotone, the soldier listening intently. Then The Pope put his hand on Mike's forehead and read something from his small Bible. He snapped the cover shut, rose and walked quickly back towards the squad, his face white and drawn. Taking his weapon from Boyd's hand, he spoke briefly to Sergeant Hardin.

"I did what I could. The rest, someone else will have to do."

Shoulders dropping, his rifle dangling loosely from his hand, The Pope walked away. The others stood in stony silence. Olive Oyl and Dancer voted with their feet and trudged after The Pope. Kuhn just kicked at the ground, avoiding everyone else's eyes.

It was Hardin who spoke.

"Gimme yo' forty-five," he said, his outstretched palm extended toward Kuhn. It was passed over, butt first. Hardin operated the slide and checked that the safety was off.

"If dis is what leadership is, dey can

fuggin' well keep it," he muttered.

They watched as he walked quickly to the soldier's side, knelt down and asked him something. Mike nodded. Hardin put the pistol to the man's temple. The others looked away. One shot.

They still had the problem of how to recover the body.

"Where's dat little shit of an interpreter?" Hardin shouted at a cluster of men near the landing zone. "Youngblade, yo' find dat little bastard and bring him over here. Jap, bring dem two prisoners."

It took Youngblade ten minutes to find the Vietnamese soldier. No one knew his real name; he was simply called "Chewie." Barely more than five feet tall, in his oversized fatigues he looked like a boy playing at war. Nor did he have any zeal for fighting. He always hid during a battle and emerged only when he thought it was safe. However, when it came to abusing prisoners, Chewie was a real zealot.

When Jap herded the two Viet Cong prisoners into sight, Chewie began a torrent of verbal abuse amid much kicking and slapping. Their hands had been secured behind them with common wire and they could not ward off the blows. The old man looked like a beaten old hound, eyes imploring for understanding. The young V.C. radiated hatred and defiance.

"Knock it off," Hardin said, lifting Chewie off the ground with his massive hand. "Yo' tell dem what I want done. Yo' tell dem to go over dere, cut the wires and bring dat body over here. Understand?"

The interpreter looked at the body of the soldier and quickly realized what the wires meant. He had seen such displays before. The idea delighted him. In a torrent of words and gestures, he told the prisoners their task. They did not move. Chewie struck the old man in the head, knocking him to the ground. Several kicks followed. The young prisoner was able to duck a kick aimed at his stomach and landed a solid kick of his own that knocked Chewie sideways. The American soldiers laughed at the interpreter's plight. Chewie did not share the merriment.

Chewie struck both prisoners viciously with his rifle butt, drawing blood with each blow, and screamed a long series of commands at them. The man seemed out of control. Boyd thought it might be better to send all three to get blown up.

"They say no." Chewie finally reported to Sergeant Hardin. "They say they be killed. Body will...uh...explode."

"Yeah, and dey did it," Hardin replied. He walked up to the old man, lying on his right side. Hardin still had Kuhn's forty-five. He laid it on the bloodied bridge of the man's nose, between his eyes. The other squad members moved from behind the man, out of the line of fire.

"Chewie, tell him he can do what I told him to do or I will blow his brains out right now," Hardin said. The guerrilla might not have understood English but he grasped full well the meaning and the deadly intention of the speaker. He began talking like a magpie, chattering in a voice that rose and fell in a sing-song, pleading manner. Chewie interpreted as fast as he could.

"He say he cannot. He say no V.C. He just farmer. V.C. come to his village, make him go with them. V.C. say..."

The discussion was ended by the thunder of the heavy handgun. The man's head snapped backward from the force of the bullet smashing through bone. It flew apart like an overripe melon, chunks of bone and brain flying through the air. The corpse sagged into a heap. Hardin walked to the second prisoner, seated on the ground.

"Now Chewie," he said quietly, "tell dis little hardass shit the same thing. I doan want no long conversation."

Chewie's eyes sparkled with delight. His body almost vibrated with pleasure as he repeated the instructions. The prisoner started to say something in reply but, glancing at the body of the dead man, he stopped talking. He stood up and turned to have the common wire cut away.

Hardin slashed through the wire with his hunting knife, opening a long gash on the man's wrist at the same time. He then jerked the V.C. around and shoved the knife into his hand, the forty-five carefully leveled at his head to dissuade any thoughts of stabbing the sergeant. It was unlikely considering the odds: a giant black soldier, standing a foot taller than his enemy, outweighing him by more than one hundred pounds, a gun against a knife.

Jap kept his rifle trained on the man's back in case he tried to run away.

The V.C. studied the body momentarily, then set about cutting the wires that were fastened to the wrists and ankles. The razor-sharp blade cut easily through the strands. Having completed that task, the guerrilla looked back at the Americans, wondering what to do next.

"Tell him to drag the body over here,"

Hardin said to Chewie, who dutifully shouted out the order.

With a shrug, the man took hold of the soldier's ankles and tugged. At first, he could not move it. Alive, the soldier had been nearly twice his weight. Now, at a dead weight, the difference was even greater. The small man pulled and tugged, dug in his feet as best he could and yanked. To no avail.

Sergeant Hardin suddenly took the M-16 from Jap's hands and fired a burst of four rounds that smacked into the ground near the guerrilla's feet. The message was clear.

The guerrilla doubled his efforts and the body began to slide slowly across the ground.

They weren't sure if there was one explosion or two. The earth beneath the body suddenly leaped skyward amidst much smoke and debris. The Viet Cong was blown into the air and came crashing down twenty feet from where he had been standing. Pieces of Private Michael H. Riley were scattered over a wide radius. There would be nothing but a few parts to send home. Where Mike had been lying, there was a black crater more than a foot deep.

"Maybe now you know what I mean

when I say a dink's life don't mean nothing," Jap said softly to Boyd.

The arrival of the medical evacuation helicopters brought their attention back to more pressing matters. Arguments broke out over who would be flown out first. Wop played it strictly by the book and Captain Adams backed him up. Those who were not in critical danger would wait. Those who were terminal and unlikely to survive would wait. First out would be those who were borderline, for whom time was critical.

A soldier with a large bandage over the top of his head and across his eyes lay on the ground, smoking a cigarette held by his buddy. A bullet had passed through his head, directly behind the eyes, entering the left temple and exiting the right. He was blind but seemed to have his mental faculties. Wop designated him for the third chopper. He died while they were loading the second. He made no sound. His chin dropped and he was gone.

The men of the fourth platoon introduced Boyd to their brand of psychological warfare. They were walking around with playing cards in their hands, putting a single card on each Viet Cong body. Sensing Boyd's curiosity, a soldier grinned through the grime and sweat and held up his deck with the cards fanned. They were all the same card.

"Dinks are superstitious as hell," the soldier explained. "They like to gamble. They know the Ace of Spades is the dead man's hand."

Boyd examined the deck. The cards had been made by the Bicycle Card Company and instead of the usual deck of cards in the box, there were fifty-two black aces.

"When they come back to pick up these bodies, the cards scare the shit out of them," the soldier said confidently. "Actually, I have my own way of doing it."

To demonstrate, the soldier used his foot to flip a corpse on to its back, then put a card on the dead man's forehead. He straightened up and took aim with a pistol. The loud report startled other soldiers who suddenly grasped their weapons and looked for the unseen enemy.

"See," the soldier said, tugging at the card which was now firmly stuck to the skull, a black hole through the center. "Works like a big ol' stapler."

The soldiers were collecting weapons in a large pile near the demolished ARVN headquarters building. Boyd picked up an

AK-47 and examined it. It felt heavy and rattled when he shook it. Jap had already picked up a similar weapon and gave Boyd some advice.

"If you want that, hide it," Jap advised. "We're supposed to send all captured weapons to Army Intelligence at Division Headquarters. They're supposed to analyze the stuff, then return them to us. Trouble is, we never see them again. Those goddam house cats and REMF's back at Bearcat keep them or sell them. The bastards sell the AK-47's to the fly boys at Bien Hoa for $250 each."

It was nearly 1600 hours when the remainder of the company was flown out. Boyd retrieved his AK-47 seconds before jumping into the chopper. He saw that most of the other men in the squad had done the same thing. Two platoons of ARVN marines arrived to finish the work of cleaning up the camp. Nearly three hundred guerrillas had been killed and the U.S. Command in Saigon would soon drop leaflets claiming that the Viet Cong leadership had not only suffered a tremendous defeat but had lied to their men that they could defeat the Americans in a pitched battle.

But if this was an American victory, it

was a costly one: nineteen men dead, another thirty-two wounded. Four American advisers who had been in the camp were never found.

They returned to the firebase filthy, parched and exhausted. The men hardly spoke, just lay about in what shade they could find, each lost in his own thoughts and memories. Boyd retrieved his diary from its hiding place and tried to put so many thoughts and feelings into words that very little of what he wrote made sense.

He wiped the mud and sweat from his hand and forearm so he would not dirty the pages. The pen felt like a foreign object in his hand and his fingers seemed numb. He started to write three times, then stopped as images flooded uncontrollably into his mind.

Day 356. I have seen, heard, smelled and tasted things today that I did not believe possible. I wish I could describe it but I think there are two vocabularies. The first is what I think, so full of horror and disgust. But when I try to describe it on paper, my second vocabulary takes over and I can't put anything into words. It seems so harmless and insignificant. We won a vic-

tory. We recaptured a stinking bit of mud from the enemy. Surely it was not worth one American life, let alone twenty. Madeira was wounded. He may be lucky. The wound looks like a ticket home. I did something stupid, went to pull a wounded man from the mud. I really don't know why. I don't know if I went to get the radio or the man. Lieutenant Brummel was blown away. It could have been any one of us. I didn't know the man at all. Did he have a family? What will they think of a headless corpse? It happened so fast, I saw many dead Viet Cong and felt nothing. It doesn't bother me. The sight of dead Americans tears me up inside. Why should I care? They could be men I would intensely dislike. I don't know them and don't want to. Maybe I just keep thinking that someday I will be among them. It can't go like this every day. If it does, the company will be wiped out in a month. Coming back in the chopper, I made a resolution. I am going to stay alive. I never thought about if before but I now know that I really want to live. I don't care what it takes or how many people I have to kill. I'm going home in 356 days. What Jap told me makes sense. My life is precious, a dink's life has no value at all.

Chapter 2
BROWN WATER NAVY

DAY 340. Since the battle in the Rung Sat there has been a period of nothingness. The artillery fires its quota of shells and we search nameless hamlets looking for the enemy. The people stare at us with expressionless, dead eyes. Yet my guess is they have practiced hiding their hatred. Charlie is avoiding us for now. The heat seems to be rising by the day. I have never known anything like it. Each breath feels like sucking in a bit of hell. It's boring but every day of boredom is one less day in Slopeland. I'm starting to have trouble with my feet. The skin between my toes is rotting. They smell awful. Nothing seems to help. I think this is the worst-smelling place in the world. It's the ugliest, too. The people look like little shriveled up monkeys to me.

The American command seemed either unable or unwilling to follow up the smashing blow given to the Viet Cong. Both sides acted like punch-drunk fighters, circling, eyeing each other but un-enthused about resuming the battle. The war became a series of small incidents.

Typical of the problems the Americans faced was the constant probing and tampering with the perimeter of the firebase. Their defenses were steadily improved. A minefield was laid in front of rows of concertina wire covered with automatic weapons, mortar registration points and the direct fire of heavy weapons. Air protection was readily available. It would take a determined force to make any dent in those defenses.

This combination should have deterred any guerrilla. Yet, never a night or day passed without an incident. A sniper had the annoying habit of taking long-range shots at soldiers walking about. The danger was present at all times, as the marksman chose different hours and positions. He was obviously equipped with a very good weapon because he was shooting at a range of 600 yards or more. The weapon had an infra-red scope, flash suppresser and silencer. One day the shot might come from a cluster of trees; the next night from somewhere in the rice paddies. The sniper managed to shoot the First Sergeant of the artillery battery in the butt. Using the latrine had become a special adventure. It was there a soldier from fourth platoon was shot in the hand as he reached for a roll of paper. Ambushes were attempted but the sniper avoided them. A special two-man sniper team was brought in to locate their nemesis but they were never able to get a glimpse of the elusive guerrilla. They never knew what became of him. One day the shooting stopped as if the marksman became bored with the game.

In addition to the sniper, they were harassed by a sapper who had taken to stealing Claymore mines from the perimeter. The mines were placed no more than fifty feet in front of the bunkers, behind rows of concertina. The Americans hung C-ration cans on the wire with pieces of metal inside the cans, expecting that any movement would cause a rattling noise. Despite these efforts, a guerrilla had crawled silently through the wire, avoided the trip flares, cut the wires leading to the mines, then removed them. The thefts had to be stopped.

Hardin and Jap devised a trap. They

removed all the Claymore mines except two. Anti-personnel mines were placed in the ground directly below where the Claymores would be positioned. The Claymore was fastened to a heavy piece of wood that was placed on the detonators of the buried mines. The plan was simple: Whoever picked up a Claymore would set off the mine buried beneath it.

Two nights passed without incident and the inventors began to suspect that their trap was too obvious. They maintained a silent vigil in their bunkers as they scanned the open fields with Starlite scopes and infra-red viewers. On the third night, their patience was rewarded.

At approximately 0300 hours, a powerful explosion woke everyone in the firebase. Men grabbed weapons and positioned themselves for a fight. But the explosion was a singular one and the next morning they discovered the results of their handiwork.

Where a Claymore had been placed, there was now a small crater, blackened earth and a partially-dismembered body. The patrol sent to investigate found the corpse lying face-down, both arms missing. When they flipped the body over, they guessed that the notorious sapper had been a small, Vietnamese girl. Much of the upper body and face had been blown away so the curious soldiers cut away the black pajama bottoms to confirm their theory. They could not know her age but she probably had been no older then ten or twelve. With a hip girth of no more than twenty inches, coated with grease, she had been ideally suited to wiggle through the wire without making a sound. They shook their heads in admiration of her courage.

"My kid sister is afraid of the dark. She has to have a night light in her bedroom. She won't go out at night, period," Kuhn said. "Do something like this? Never."

"Goddam people are crazy," Knowles added.

They enlarged the crater and buried the body right there. They discussed some sort of marker but decided not to bother.

As the dry season intensified, the sun bore down mercilessly and the men sought every possible relief. The tracks had no air conditioning systems but they were equipped with standard heaters. When they had to be inside the vehicles, the men ran the heaters. It was actually cooler than sitting in the stale, super-heated air. The temperature reached 110 degrees by 1000 hours. The heat came down like a giant electric blanket, struck the parched, dusty ground, then bounced back up. The slightest physical activity produced profuse sweating and fatigue. Boyd suffered worse than the other men as his blood had not yet thinned sufficiently to adjust to the climate. They drank anything and everything. When supply helicopters arrived ferrying ammunition, food and water, the chopper crews would also have cases of Filipino San Miguel and Korean Lucky Tiger beer stacked on the floor. Over the sound of turning blades, the grunts would shout and make hand gestures to bargain for the prized booty. No price would have been too high for the parched soldiers, although the Korean beer was aptly described as hippo piss.

When they weren't patrolling, the men played cards, read the Stars and Stripes newspaper, listened to music on the armed forces network and tried to sleep. Boyd found it difficult to write anything meaningful in his diary.

Day 332. This is the Land that Time Forgot. When nothing is happening, you wish there was something to do. Then, when the shit hits the fan, you long for moments of boredom. Everyone is temperamental and edgy. Something is really bothering Knowles. We give him his privacy. He stays by himself most of the time. Dancer and Olive Oyl got into a fight over nothing. Jap had to break it up. It's the heat. They say it is going to get even hotter. Hard to believe. The only good thing is that we get more A-rats than before.

At night, they were soaked with a heavy dew that made them shiver. Although the temperature did not drop much below seventy degrees, the effect was as chilling as a winter wind. They wrapped themselves in poncho liners and strained to see though the heavy mist that settled over the fields. In the morning, they wiped rivulets of condensation from their weapons and equipment and tried to dry out.

As Jap had predicted, Boyd never felt dry. Long before the morning sun had baked the dew from his uniform, he would start to sweat. He developed rashes everywhere skin touched skin: armpits, crotch, behind his knees. Whenever possible, the men walked around in rubber shower clogs while rows of unlaced, muddy boots lined the tops of their bunkers.

And there was the smell. Everything

and everyone exuded a stench. The combined scents of sweat, human waste, cordite, fuel exhaust, rotting flesh, rice paddies fertilized by water buffalo dung and a thousand other offensive things was overpowering. When one man stood up, another lay down in his filth and sweat and tried to sleep.

Every third day mail bags arrived by helicopter and the news from home was devoured. The men traditionally sat in a small pow-wow circle, eyes protected from the glare by cheap Post Exchange plastic sunglasses, a communal case of beer in the center, and read their letters over and over again. This was a sweet and sour time. It was their lifeline to sanity but crudely reminded them of where they were and what they were missing.

Knowles had a teenage, pregnant wife who wrote him long letters every day. They had impulsively married when he got his orders for Vietnam, convincing themselves that it would be better to have a just a few weeks together than none at all. She lived with her parents and worked at a low-paying job in a department store. She wrote on onionskin paper. The letters were so thick they constantly split the sides of the envelopes. She said the paper wasn't perfumed but it reeked of something that spread like a gas attack when he unfolded the pages. It contrasted so much with their own stench the effect was magnified one hundred times. Although he prized her letters, the men could see that he was very troubled by her constant whimpering about how she worried, cried and anguished that he might be killed without ever having seen their child. The doctor said she might worry herself into a miscarriage. After reading her letters, he would say nothing for hours.

Olive Oyl received so many letters from drinking buddies, horny girls and relatives that they suggested he should have his own APO number. Dancer had to move his lips to read and sometimes had to ask someone to read certain words to him. He particularly liked the letters from collection agencies threatening civil action. He was the king of impulsive buyers. He owed a jeweler $1,500 for a diamond tie clip which he managed to buy on credit while unemployed.

Jap had two sisters who wrote to him nearly every day. Chatty, long letters about ordinary things in a world that seemed so unreal. They wanted to know why they hadn't seen him on the television news.

Boyd's mother wrote short, boring letters describing earth-shaking events such as a dead car battery and old Mr. Thomas developing a heart condition. She stuffed the envelopes with clippings from the local newspaper, complete with her explanatory notes about who the people were. Most of the news was dreary, long dissertations about who died or who was ill. Stephanie wrote to him once, describing all the cool college guys who were after her. She added that she had joined an antiwar organization and hoped he would do the right thing by refusing to fight against "people fighting for their national liberation." He never answered the letter.

The Pope seldom received letters. Communication was done by sending cassette tapes back and forth. He listened to the tapes with a small earplug that connected to a portable player that ate flashlight batteries faster than the commo section could get new ones.

Photos were important to their moral and most of the men had their own Japanese cameras purchased in the PX at giveaway prices. They sent the film rolls home in packages marked "Film-Do Not Xray." The postal service now regularly passed mail through xray machines after it was learned that some soldiers had mailed home weapons and explosives.

"Gawd, ain't she beautiful? Look at them eyes!" Kuhn exclaimed one afternoon, holding a photo in both hands as if it was too magnificent to touch with soiled hands. He proudly showed a photo of his favorite dog and then exhausted them a long discourse about her bird-fetching abilities in any kind of weather.

Grudgingly, almost ceremonially, they burned the letters, envelopes and photographs with any names or information written on them. They knew quite clearly that the Viet Cong made propaganda from captured materials taken from the bodies of American soldiers. It was not uncommon for them to be smuggled to anti-war groups in the United States and used to harass the families of men killed in action. They did not want to burn these things but they knew it was something they had to do to protect their families. But each time they burned their letters they cut the ties once again. Here and now, in this place, there was no such place as home. This was home and they were family.

Equally important to the letters were the food parcels. Each man had implored family members to send anything edible that could survive the heat. Parcels arrived containing vacuum-packed meats, cheeses and crackers. They savored boxes of minute rice, miniature bottles of whiskey like the ones the airlines served, foilwrapped packs of dried soups and bottles of garlic salt. They shared everything, making soup and hobo stew from these prized items, cooking the food over burning blocks of C4 explosive or a small gasoline stove. The Pope's mother mailed a huge Lebanon bologna, shaped like a football, packed in dry, stale popcorn. They cut it into chunks and ate it in five minutes, then they ate the popcorn covered with onion salt.

Youngblade never received any mail. He did not seem to resent that the others did, and no one asked him about it. Not everyone had a family. He just drank his beer and listened as the others shared those things that were not too personal, looking at the others with intense, black eyes that seemed so intelligent and yet so secretive. Youngblade never wore sunglasses and didn't squint no matter how bright the sunlight. His eyes were like two black coals hidden behind the high cheekbones. He had a noble face, almost arrogant. One of

Jap's sisters offered to write to him but he declined. No one was certain whether he could read or write.

Nine days after the battle for the ARVN camp, a replacement arrived for Madiera. Boyd had hoped that when this day arrived, he could shed his F.N.G. title. He was sorely disappointed, for the man wasn't new to Vietnam at all. He was serving a second tour and more astonishing, he had volunteered for it.

Private Larry Moore, a tall, muscular man with a mop of blonde hair that was almost white, was twenty-four years old, a senior citizen by Vietnam standards. There was a bald strip along the side of his head where hair refused to grow over a patch of scar tissue. Moore explained that a bullet had punched through the right side of his helmet, then whirled around inside a dozen times before exiting through the same hole.

Moore had served a full tour with the 25th Infantry Division based at Cu Chi. He had taken his discharge and tried to integrate back into civilian life. Sitting cross-legged, he talked to the other squad members as if he had known them for years.

"I went back to my home town," he explained as he expertly removed the lid from a can of fruit cocktail with the little P38 on his dog tag chain, "found my Old Lady living with another guy. Okay, shit happens. I got my old job back-cause they have to hire you back under federal law-but under a different supervisor. A big, pig-faced lard-ass. A real ugly dickhead. Right off, he started calling me 'Hero.' It wasn't a compliment. He never let up. He rode me all the time."

"So, quit. Quit the goddam job," Kuhn interrupted as he scraped the last of ham and lima beans from a can. "Go somewhere else. Lay on the beach and get stoned. You don't come back here."

"There's more," Moore insisted, his voice taking on insistent, solemn tone. "It isn't the...same...back there. Things have changed. Half the country is rioting. Blacks are burning down cities. Students are burning down the universities. Man, never tell anyone you've been to 'Nam.' Your sister will spit on you. I just didn't fit in. None of my so-called friends would have anything to do with me. It's supposed to be the era of Free Love. The hippies all love each other but they don't love you. This is ironic-Charlie is their hero. They love Luke-the-Gook but they don't love you. There's no parade waiting for you."

"Don't want no parade," Dancer insisted. "But there ain't nothing in the world that would make me come back here."

"That's what I once thought," Moore continued, drinking the last of the fruit cocktail from the can, then tucking the plastic spoon into his shirt pocket. "But one day it came to me. When I was over here, I was somebody. I did my job and men respected me for it. No one messed with me. I had responsibility. I was doing something. Back at my old job, I was nothing, doing nothing, for nothing. I wanted to come back here. I had a feeling of unfinished business. And here I felt I was among my own people."

The other squad members listened intently, eyes pointed towards the ground, the ashes of their photos and letters in front of them. The thought of going home was everything and now Moore was telling them it was a lie. There was nothing to go home to. They were like astronauts stranded forever on a distant planet.

"The next day," Moore continued, "I walked into the plant and my supervisor called me 'Hero' and I kicked the shit out of him. I really did a job on him. I hated him ten times more than I ever hated

Charlie. Then I took off before the cops got there. The recruiting station was the last place in the world they would look for me."

Although the squad members figured Moore was possibly deranged, Jap was pleased he didn't have to train a totally new recruit. Hardin didn't bother the man with the usual orientation routine. Moore had never fought in the rice paddies but had plenty of experience in jungle fighting. He would sometimes describe the problems the 25th had encountered and the other men would listen with keen interest. It was information they might need some day.

If the movers and shakers at MACV in Saigon believed the Viet Cong had suddenly lost their backbone, they erred. Ten days after the battle for the ARVN camp, the guerrillas targeted a 50-man Vietnamese Government Pacification Team for annihilation. The team drove into a small hamlet near Rach Bai, set up a projector and loudspeaker and tried to re-educate the people. They were supposed to be protected by a company of ARVN Rangers that never showed up. After a wasted two hours, they gave the villagers Japanese radios to listen to Saigon Radio, packed up and tried to drive back to their base at Cay Lai, following the exact same route. The Viet Cong ambushed them a mile from the hamlet and killed the entire team in a ten-minute turkey shoot. When the ARVN Rangers were finally dispatched to see what had become of the missing team, they were ambushed and lost twenty of their own men.

American intelligence officers concluded that the 514th V.C. Regiment had received new Chicom weapons and was now flexing its muscles. The 514th called a peculiar bend in the Mekong River "home." The Americans nicknamed this expanse of marsh "Snoopy's Nose." In ten years of fighting, the ARVN had never been able to take one inch of that impenetrable fortress from the enemy. MACV decided it was time to end that situation.

"It don't look good, brothers," Olive Oyl shook his head as the squad stood along the bank of a narrow river that fed its brown water into the Mekong. They had been airlifted to this collection point that morning and were now waiting to be picked up by units of the Riverine Force.

"It never looks good," Kuhn retorted. "Damn, we're walking again. We're mech infantry and we're always humping instead of riding."

The company had been chosen to beef up the force which would attack the V.C. in their haven. Captain Adams had been replaced by the company executive officer, Lieutenant Phelps. Hardin had temporarily become company 'first shirt.'

"What the Keee-rist is that?" Dancer suddenly asked.

They stared at the apparitions approaching them. A flotilla of strange vessels came chugging up the river. In the lead were two "Monitors"- armored assault boats with turrets bristling with guns. They looked like floating rafts with tin cans glued to the deck. Behind them, moving in single file, were six LST landing barges, their high profiles concealing the men of the 3/60th infantry, veterans of riverine warfare. The force was based aboard the troop ship, USS Benewah, anchored in the Mekong Basin.

The armada moved slowly past where the men waited on the bank. Boyd could see men in flak jackets manning 50-caliber machine guns. Others were scanning the river banks with binoculars. The infantry "grunts" were concealed behind the high sides of the barges.

The last two LST's in the column suddenly swung towards the shore, a crewman waving for them to make a landing
space. With a grinding lurch, the crafts
dragged bottom. Their ramps came down
with a sudden splash, revealing the empty
innards of the vessels.

"Are we supposed to get in this thing?"
The Pope asked. "I didn't join no goddam
navy."

"Move it!" Hardin shouted, dividing the
men into two groups. "Sit along the sides,
face in."

In single file, their boots banging on
the steel ribs of the ramp, the soldiers
trooped into the belly of the beast and sat
down. Sandbags lined the bottom but the
hot metal along the sides seared any exposed skin. They could no longer see anything but the sky and each other. On the
rear bulkhead someone had painted:

~~Kill for freedom~~
~~Kill for peace~~
Kill for fun.

The ramp rose with a loud grinding
sound and the vessel's powerful motor
drew them out onto the river. Dancer was
genuinely distressed.

"What if this thing sinks? I can't swim.
Who knows what's in that water? I've

heard there are poisonous snakes in the river."

The other men shared Dancer's misgivings. Although the sides of the craft were nearly a foot thick, much of that was just air between metal plates. A Viet Cong on the riverbank could lob a rifle grenade into the middle of the craft with potentially devastating results. The Pope stood up and peered over the side. A crewman behind a machine gun shouted for him to sit down. The Pope made an obscene gesture and stayed where he was.

"Screw this," Moore said. "I want to see who's shooting at me."

He, too, stood up and shoved his rifle barrel over the side of the landing barge. Metal poles with a single strand of rope ran around the boat just over their heads.

The trapped feeling was infectious and within seconds all the men were on their feet, facing outward. The crewman shouted at them again but they ignored him.

The river was approximately 150 yards wide. Both banks were covered with a dense green foliage of trees and bushes that could conceal a hundred guerrillas. The water was calm, its dark brown color churned up by the prow of the boat into a white lather. The throb of the motor was the only sound they heard. They could see the other boats in a single line ahead of them. Behind them was another armored monitor, its turrets pointed towards the river banks, an American flag flapping in the air. It was terribly hot and the metal of the barge reflected the heat back into their bodies like a mirror. They pushed their helmets back and wiped sweat from their faces with the green towels wrapped around their necks. They began taking small drinks of the Kool Aid in their canteens.

"I can't believe I'm doing this," Moore said in a low voice to Youngblade. "We're ducks in a shooting gallery."

Twenty minutes after boarding the ship, the river suddenly became more narrow and the position of the sun told them they were now going north. The lead Monitor began to fire its machine guns at abandoned, fallen-down hootches along the bank and any place that might provide ambush cover. Gunners on the LST did the same thing.

The lead vessel suddenly shot out a powerful stream of flame that engulfed a tall tree close to the river. The soldiers watched in quiet awe as the vegetation vanished in a chimney of fire. Most impressive was the range of the flame thrower. It shot the burning liquid more than seventy yards.

The lead ship also shot at everything floating in the waterlogs, old C-ration boxes, dead animals. The Viet Cong were adept at manufacturing and disguising floating mines. A harmless-looking tuft of grass might conceal one of their devices.

They chugged up river for another thirty minutes without any sign of the enemy. At a spot where the river bank seemed cut away, creating a wider expanse of water, the barges suddenly turned sharply towards the shore and crunched along the river bottom. They stopped with a lurch.

"Let's go. Move out!" Hardin shouted as the ramp dropped heavily into the mud, leaving the soldiers a gap of ten feet of brown mire to wade through.

Boyd had thought the area around the ARVN camp was the worst terrain possible. The marshes proved him wrong. He had trouble finding anything solid at all and for a moment thought he was in quicksand. The marsh was covered by a foot of water with small, prominent rises of tufted wild grass every few feet. But when he tried to walk on these high points they simply gave way, sending him flailing to one side or the other. With his thirty-pound rucksak on his back and his flak jacket, he felt he was sinking deeper with each step.

Several men fell, twisting their arms skyward in a effort to keep their rifles out of the mud and water. Others helped them to their feet.

"How are we supposed to walk in this shit?" Kuhn asked, after Youngblade and Olive Oyl pulled him to his feet. He was mud-covered to his neck.

"Goddamit, spread out!" Jap ordered. "Stop playing grab-ass and keep your distance."

The men tried to comply with the order but could not. The marsh was full of deep holes and when a man stepped into one, he sank to his chest. He was imprisoned there until others pulled him free.

The heat was unrelenting and tempers rose quickly. It took tremendous effort to move a single foot. They felt imprisoned in goo. Sometimes two men went down together, clinging to each other for support that wasn't there.

"Fuck this!" Knowles shouted, after falling for the third time. His M-60 was unrecognizable for the crap layering on it. The ammunition belt wasn't visible at all. "I say we go back to the river."

"Keep moving," Hardin said over and over again to small groups of men who had come to a dead stop. There wasn't much fire in his voice. His own mood was dark and gloomy. They were sitting ducks, out in the open, unable to move at more than a snail's pace.

They had progressed less than one hundred yards from the river. Their objective, a cluster of thatched huts and trees believed to be a Viet Cong headquarters, was still another two hundred yards away. To their left they could see men of the 60th making somewhat better progress. They had experience working in the Delta and had fastened themselves together with long ropes looped around their waists. Each man tried to keep the rope taunt as they pulled each other through the muck. If a man fell, the rope line supported him.

"Well, that's just swell," Jap said, after watching the procedure. "How do you fight if everyone is tied together?"

From the distant trees, a Viet Cong sniper put the question to a proper field test. They heard a loud report and a man from the 60th fell into the muck. The other men pulled a loop in the rope at their waists and their ropes suddenly fell away.

Hardin's nightmare came true. They could not run and there was no place to hide.

"Suppressing fire!" Lieutenant Phelps ordered. "Burn their asses!"

The men instinctively squatted down into the water and mud. Their rifles were above water but their ammunition pouches were submerged. Knowles' M-60 quickly jammed and he worked furiously to try to clear it. Some M-16's opened up and Youngblade was able to pop an M-79 grenade which fell short of the tree line, splashing harmlessly into the muck.

From a bunker hidden by one of the hootches, a Viet Cong machine gun suddenly opened up, sending the men diving deeper into the water. Mercifully, the gunner was an amateur, firing long bursts that punched holes into the sky many feet over their heads. The squad submerged themselves to their noses, trying to be invisible. Once again, the radio was their only possible salvation.

Boyd could hear Lieutenant Phelps calling for an air strike. The commander of one of the Monitors heard the firing and brought his ship to a point a few yards from where they had disembarked. The 50-caliber machine guns began firing at the hootches with steady, powerful bursts. But as soon as the guns suppressed one enemy position, another seemed to appear.

"Go back to the river!" Phelps ordered, but no one moved. Retreat was just as impossible as advance.

Boyd fired his rifle three times and emptied the magazine. He groped around in the water until he was able to pull a full magazine from his pouch. It slipped through his fingers and vanished. He found another, holding on to it as tightly as he could. He needed three hands. He could not open the protective sandwich bag with one hand and there was no place to put his rifle down. He finally laid the M-16 across his left shoulder and balanced it with his arm while he used his hands to open the bag. He never finished the task.

A bullet struck the plastic hand grip of his rifle. Pieces of plastic and bullet fragments struck the side of his helmet, knocking him to the right. The rifle landed two feet behind him and quickly sank out of sight.

Strong hands pulled him up and shoved his helmet back on his head.

Muddy water ran down him face. There was a ringing in his ears and a pounding in his head. He couldn't keep his balance.

"Boyd! You hit?" Kuhn asked.

"Dunno," he mumbled as he groped around for his rifle.

"Stay down," Kuhn insisted, pushing him into the mud to his chin. Although he held his shotgun out of the water, it was useless at such a long range.

The enemy fire was concentrated most heavily upon the men of the 60th who were considerably closer to the well-prepared enemy bunkers. In the first ten minutes, half of the men of two platoons had been killed or wounded.

They heard the crash of a heavy weapon behind them, then turned just in time to see the Monitor burst into flames. A second belch of fire from the opposite bank announced the news: a recoiless rifle had blown the side out of the ship. It was listing to one side, black smoke and orange fire pouring from a dozen places. The surviving crew threw off their flak jackets and jumped into the water.

"They're on the other bank! They're behind us!" Moore shouted. "We can't go forward or back."

"Cover them!" Phelps screamed, pointing at the men swimming away from the ship. "Burn the other bank!"

A few men with operating weapons tried to comply but the effect was weak. M-16's full of mud do not operate. Knowles was the only one able to contribute anything. He finally got the M-60 to fire short bursts before it seized up. He cleared the weapon again and again. Despite the blockages, it kept working.

The larger picture was starting to develop. The Viet Cong had constructed their defenses in an elaborate ring of interlocking positions. They had taken advantage of every natural piece of camouflage and had dug out deep bunkers with special ditches to keep out the water. They were dry and their weapons worked. Each gun had its assigned fields of fire. They were playing on their home turf.

The Americans had little to fight with except their air force. Phelps was talking to the FAC, the radio half immersed in water as the operator tried to hunker down like everyone else. The Lieutenant's voice was hesitant and confused as he tried to direct the jets to every target at once. Circling above them, the FAC sounded infuriatingly calm and businesslike. Did he have any idea of what it was like on the ground?

"Tamale FAC, what can you give me? Go," Phelps asked.

"I have napalm, CBU's, twenty-mike-mike. Go," the pilot's voice crackled through the radio.

"Napalm!" Phelps latched on the word as if it were divine deliverance. "Along the tree line. The hootches. The bank. Along the opposite bank."

"Uh...roger. Pop smoke," the FAC requested.

The first smoke grenade just sank in the mud. The second wouldn't work at all. The third Phelps just held in his hand until it got too hot, then he tossed it into the air. The FAC saw it.

The first of the jets appeared from the west, racing over the fields less than two hundred feet from the ground. The men saw it clearly, an F-4 with lumpy attachments fastened to the wings and belly. It looked like an overloaded bat, a dark avenging angel.

Boyd saw the large canister separate from the plane and tumble earthward. A ball of orange flame suddenly engulfed the greenery that shrouded their tormentors. It seemed to start at the western edge of the trees, then spread like a giant prairie fire for more than fifty yards. The fire ball jumped higher than the tree tops, crackling and roaring as the burning napalm rose to 600 degrees. To the soldiers pinned down in the fields, it was an unfolding red rose.

Phelps was talking more calmly, directing the jets towards the hootches and the opposite bank. He ordered what remained of the company to fall back to the riverbank. The enemy fire was diminished but never stopped.

The 60th had recklessly called for a medevac helicopter. It could not possibly land in the mud and trying to lift wounded up to a hovering ship would have been tortuous. Nor was the battle over.

Dustoff crews have one great fault. They never say no. They would attempt rescues that bordered on suicide and it was wrong to ask them to do it.

The pilot held the craft very still, just a foot above the mud, the prop churning the water into waves. Three men tried to drag a wounded buddy to the open doorway. Even the most nearsighted Viet Cong couldn't have missed such a target and nearly every gun was turned on it.

Small arms and automatic weapons punched holes through the chopper in such numbers that pieces of hot metal were flying around inside like popcorn. Every member of the crew was hit by something. A 51-caliber machine gun needed only one long burst to take off most of the tail. With a lurch, the machine swung wildly in a 180-degree arch, then smashed into the field. The pilot and one crewman crawled out of the wreck. The others were no where to be seen.

The air force gave all that it could. Before the first flight had to return to base, the second was on station. The FAC could see very well the situation below. The jets bombed, strafed and fried every position where the enemy could be hidden. But as soon as one position fell silent, another seemed to spring up.

The company was crawling slowly, doggedly back to the river. They had no contact with the 60th, whose radio had ceased operating. There was no plan, they just banded together in two's and three's and tried to fend for themselves.

Boyd, Kuhn and Dancer were within a few feet of each other and formed a loosely-knit team. Two men would try to make their weapons fire while the third crawled a few yards.

Helicopter gunships appeared and began shooting up the enemy positions on the opposite bank, working east to west. Each time they made a pass, the V.C. fire stopped. It resumed almost immediately. The Viet Cong could not leave their concealed positions. They would fight until darkness and then perhaps slip away.

When Dancer fell heavily into the water, Boyd instinctively knew he had been hit. He shouted to Kuhn and they thrashed through the water to pull the man from the brown soup. When they got his face out of the water, blood was rushing from the base of his neck. The bullet had gone through the back and out the front. The hole in the rear was large, the hole in the front massive.

Dancer flung his arms about, reaching for anything for support. Boyd tried to stem the flow of blood with a compress bandage. He achieved little, trying to affix a mud soaked, wet piece of cloth to a gaping wound. Kuhn held Dancer in a one-armed bear hug, but almost immediately, a bullet struck his hand, tearing his shotgun from his grasp. He looked down and saw the bloody stump where his little finger had been. He shook his hand as if the shake the pain away.

"The fucker shot me," he said in a matter-of-fact, calm manner.

Boyd placed his right hand against Dancer's throat and pressed firmly to try to stop the bleeding, trying to remember what he had been taught about pressure points. The flow of blood slowed. Against the man's mud-covered brown skin, the crimson red seemed unreal. Kuhn rescued his beloved shotgun and seemed more concerned about the smashed stock than his wound.

"Keep moving!" Phelps shouted at them.

They positioned themselves one on each side of Dancer and began a peculiar motion of half-crawling and half-swimming. The mud made an infuriating slurping sound every time they pulled the wounded man's body.

Slowly, in tiny bunches, the exhausted soldiers dragged themselves to the river bank. Units were mixed up, men could not find their squad leaders. No one knew how many were dead or wounded in the marsh. The flotilla was long gone, only the half-sunken Monitor remained of the small fleet. The top of the radio antennae protruding above the water marked its watery grave.

They could not dig holes in the muck, so they just spread out along the bank and kept a watchful eye across the river. Everyone had questions. Were they going to be picked up? Reinforced? How? When?

Hardin wanted to send some men to occupy the opposite bank but Phelps would not agree. The river was too treacherous to cross without ropes or other special equipment.

Wop was again overwhelmed by the numbers of wounded. Most of his medical supplies were wet. Bandages would not stay in place. He argued for a dustoff but Phelps refused to consider it. There could be no evacuation until the enemy was beaten or departed. That meant nightfall.

Boyd and Kuhn took turns holding a compress to Dancer's neck. Their insistent calls for a medic went unheeded. Kuhn wrapped a muddy bandage around his hand, which now throbbed and pained him greatly.

When Wop finally got to them, he took a quick look at Kuhn's hand and said he wouldn't waste morphine on it.

"Too bad it wasn't your trigger finger," he said. "Man loses his trigger finger, he goes home. Little finger don't mean shit."

He looked at Dancer's wound and the man's eyes, then showed Boyd how to correctly apply pressure to the artery. As the wounded man wasn't conscious, morphine wasn't needed.

"He's going home," Wop said, "in a bag."

The sun baked them all that day and despite their best efforts at rationing, their canteens were nearly empty. Jap and Hardin discussed the problem and decided that when darkness came they would have to try to recover canteens from their dead comrades.

"We doan get some water, we be drinking dis shit," Hardin summarized.

Water was a double-headed curse. It was ev-erywhere but men were parched. In the late afternoon, they became aware of the second problem-the tide.

The level of the river began to rise rapidly. The water, which had flowed so quietly, now began making slapping noises against the river bank. Soon it rolled over the bank and into the marshes. They had been knee deep in water. Now they were waist deep and it was still rising. They squatted in the brown lake, weapons held high, and kept a watchful eye. The air force was still pounding enemy positions on both sides of the river, but every careless move brought an instant reply from Viet Cong snipers. The enemy was subdued but he was still there.

They tried to clean their weapons but there wasn't a dry cloth anywhere. The air force-the God-blessed air force-stayed with them all day. The enemy was hunkered down deep in their holes, shooting less often. The constant aerial pounding was taking a toll on their numbers and nerves. Each side now waited for the deliverance of nightfall. The guerrillas could slip away; the Americans could collect their dead. The soldier on each side had given all that he could and owed no more.

Soldiers are soldiers but commanders are cut from a different cloth. The Viet Cong commander guessed that the American commander would reorganize his forces and at first light try to reinforce those units that had been so severely mauled. He would not expect the Viet Cong to stand and fight. Those reinforcements could be given similar treatment.

The U.S. brigade commander, in his sandbagged command post at Dong Tam, poured over the maps and reports with his staff. The operation had been a disaster from the start, but there were now opportunities. If held in place, the Viet Cong could be surrounded. Marks were made on the Plexiglass-covered maps with colored grease pencils. Another riverine landing here; airlift a company there. More arrows neatly drawn. Use all the reserves that Division Headquarters could spare. Radios crackled. The enemy would try to withdraw at night. He must not be allowed to do so. Strange names were relayed by radio, names such as "Puff," "Spooky" and "Fire Fly."

The battalion commander frowned as he looked at the developing battle plan. The grease pencils did not provide much relief for the men trapped along the river bank. He had seen their plight from the air and had talked to Phelps by radio. They were exhausted, parched and almost chest deep in water. Their weapons were filled with mud and silt.

"Sir, what about my companies?" he asked as he placed his finger on Snoopy's Nose. "They are in terrible shape. I want to try to take them out tonight."

The brigade commander did not reply for a moment but stood gazing down at the map. His Operations Officer nervously shuffled his feet and drew one more box on the plastic. There were no human faces on it, just lines, arrows and boxes. Little blue boxes meant American forces; little red boxes meant enemy forces. Good guys

and bad guys. No pictures of eighteen-
year-only kids lying face down in a cess-
pool. The brigade commander couldn't see
wounded soldiers drowning as the water
flooded the marshes and swept over them
where they lay, weighted down with their
equipment. But he knew.

"I'm sorry, Tom," the colonel said
firmly. "I need everything at my disposal
for tomorrow's battle. I cannot spare anything tonight for a rescue operation."

"We can have them out in three hours,"
the battalion commander protested.

"They stay where they are," came the
curt reply. "They are the bait. A relief operation is not what I have in mind. I in-
tend to destroy the 514th Viet Cong Regiment once and for all."

"Bait? My men are bait?"

The two professional soldiers locked
eyes. The command bunker filled with tension so thick it could be cut with a knife.
The Operations Officer suddenly found
another minor detail that needed his urgent attention elsewhere.

"Bait," was the final word.

The events of nature are not altered by
the mere presence of humans at war. The
river methodically, almost musically, con-

tinued to rise, each successive wave just a fraction higher than the one before. Long before total darkness it was completely over the bank and beyond. Squatting was no longer sufficient, the men now had to stand, the water line just below their arm pits. No one wanted to discuss the crucial question: Could the water rise over their heads?

Boyd and Kuhn took turns holding Dancer above the water level. While one held the wounded man, an arm under his chin, the other held Kuhn's shotgun out of the water. Boyd's and Dancer's M-16's were long since lost, a fact that infuriated Sergeant Hardin when he checked on Dancer's condition.

Two more hours dragged by until the sun finally began to disappear below the horizon. The men pestered platoon leaders with the same endless questions: when will we get relief and how will it come? The answer, finally received by radio, stunned them. No relief. We hang on.

Sergeant Hardin addressed the most urgent problem: the shortage of water. Men could go without food for days but water was essential for life. He persuaded Lieutenant Phelps that they had to get water from the only sure source: the canteens of the dead men left in the marshes. Any wounded man left behind had surely drowned by now. Hardin would lead a small party to find bodies and take the water. He choose Boyd, Youngblade and a soldier from another platoon who had ended up with them during the sheer confusion of the battle. Boyd suspected Hardin picked him because he was still angry about the lost rifle. Kuhn entrusted his shotgun to The Pope, who relieved him of holding Dancer's heavy form.

They formed a loose skirmish line, fifty feet apart. They took no weapons other than their knives. Each had a piece of rope to tie canteens or belts together. At 2300 hours they began to wade slowly back into the flooded expanse of the marsh.

Clouds hid the moon and stars so that Boyd could not see five feet ahead. Although they moved slowly, each step made a telltale slurping sound that Boyd was certain could be heard five miles away. At times he could not see the others and tried to keep in line with them by sound. The water felt warm, almost as if it had been heated. It also stunk of rotting vegetation.

For an hour they moved without seeing or finding anything. Boyd had just concluded it was a hopeless needle-in-ahaystack game when he stumbled over something large and bulky. He frantically lunged at whatever it was with his knife, the blade hit solid resistance. He had trouble pulling it free.

Slowly he moved his hand over the obstacle before realizing it was a human body, held under the water by the weight of equipment. He had stabbed a dead soldier.

"Boyd! Whatdahell you doin'?" he heard Sergeant Hardin hiss.

"It's okay," he whispered back.

Remembering his purpose, he groped about the lifeless body, trying to pinpoint the rucksack and belt. He could not reach the front of the belt without ducking his head underwater. After much struggling, he opened the rucksack and found what he was sure would be there: the man's third canteen. It felt full. The heft of it gave him a sense of pleasure. Nearly a full quart of life-giving water. For a moment, he wondered who the man was, then shook the thoughts from his mind. He didn't really want to know. Then he made a conscious decision, as selfish as anything he had ever done. He unscrewed the cap on the canteen and drank half the contents without pausing. It was beautiful and life-giving.

He was sure he would never take clean water for granted again. Other men needed water, too, but self-preservation had its place.

He strung a cord around the neck of the canteen, hung it over his shoulder, then began wading forward again, searching for more bodies. He felt renewed strength and vitality from the life-giving fluid.

Five minutes later, he had collected another four canteens from submerged bodies. He carefully tied them together in a string, trying to keep them from making noise by banging together. The whole operation was going well, as long as he did not think about the dead men who were unknowingly giving up their water.

In another fifteen minutes he had two more canteens, hanging them over his shoulder like a string of giant beads. Their weight gave him reassurance that the problem of thirst had been solved. Another problem had not been anticipated.

As he began probing what he thought was another body, the "corpse" suddenly moved. It more than moved-it leaped up and swung at him.

Something crashed into his left shoulder, knocking him backward. He felt a rush of water from the smashed canteen that had saved his life. He cried aloud and struggled to keep his feet.

The Viet Cong swung wildly at him again, the woosh of air from the small machete striking his ear. Boyd lunged with his knife and struck nothing. He could not see his adversary clearly. The man was nothing but a fleeting outline that kept disappearing.

Boyd strained his eyes and ears and tried to plan his next thrust with his knife. His hand was slippery and he had a dreaded fear of dropping the knife. Slowly, he circled to his right, hoping to catch even a slight glimpse of his enemy.

From just two feet away a sharp cry rang out, followed by a low groan. Then, just the plopping sound of something sinking into the mud.

"You okay?" he heard Youngblade ask quietly.

"Yeah," he stammered. "Thanks. What the hell was that?"

"Sapper," came the quick reply. "I stabbed him. Probably looking for weapons and things. Where there's one, there's more. We'd better get the hell out of here."

"I couldn't even see him," Boyd said as he felt his shoulder for any wound. There was none. He felt very weak. He was trembling as if very cold.

"City boys got no night vision," Youngblade explained. "Let's di-di."

Youngblade moved off to alert the others and Boyd gratefully began moving slowly back towards the river. At least he hoped he was going in the right direction.

It took an hour before they were challenged by the listening posts. Another fifteen minutes until they were along the river bank. Hardin took all the canteens and began rationing drinks to the men. Boyd found Dancer and Kuhn. The soldier was very tired and happy to have Boyd relieve him of the weight. He listened intently as Boyd talked about his encounter with the sapper. He still had the slashed canteen and said he was going to keep it as a souvenir.

The morning sun found the company scattered all along the river bank. At the same time the water began to recede, leaving behind men so drenched with gray mud they looked like bodies that had been dug from fresh graves.

Boyd was finally able to ease Dancer down and rest his aching arms. He seemed very still and rigid. A half hour later, Wop pronounced him dead.

"He's dead. Let him go."

"He's not dead!" Boyd replied angrily, keeping a strong grip around the man's chest. "Just do your damn job and take care of him. He's not dead!"

"He's dead," Wop insisted quietly. "You can let him go."

"You're wrong. Look at him, you miserable Dago!" Boyd shouted, his voice cracked and broken. "You think we'd hold him up all this time if he's dead?"

Wop shook his head and walked away. Later, he returned with Jap and Hardin and they finally persuaded Boyd to let Dancer go.

"Been dead for hours," the medic explained as they put the soldier into a body bag. The realization that they had been holding a dead man for hours just added to Boyd's and Kuhn's anger and fatigue.

"I wish whoever planned this could join us, just for a little while," Kuhn said. "I'd make him eat this mud till he choked to death."

The men began agitating for relief. Lieutenant Phelps became extremely irritated, raging at each man who asked the question.

"How the fuck do I know? Do they tell me anything? We get relieved when they're good and ready."

The fact that the Viet Cong were still there was quickly apparent. Any man that stuck his head up was soon greeted by a well-aimed sniper's bullet. Occasionally, a mortar round would land nearby, doing little harm as it simply blew gobs of mud into the air. No one bothered to answer back. They were too tired to care.

At 0800 hours the air force returned, bombing and strafing the same enemy positions as the day before. Lieutenant Phelps was unable to tell them anything new.

At 1100 hours the battalion commander told him by radio a resupply would be attempted. The news shocked them. It meant there would be no relief. They were staying put.

Sergeant Hardin again argued for crossing the river but Phelps said no. The men had no strength to make such a crossing. They were nearly out of drinking water and the heat was becoming intense.

At 1200 hours a helicopter made several passes, then came down to try to drop supplies. It was greeted with Viet Cong heavy automatic weapons fire that killed a door gunner. The chopper veered sharply away.

At 1400 hours an artillery battery fired smoke shells to try to provide cover and another resupply was attempted. It had no more success than the first and fled the scene. Shortly afterward, a helicopter tried to drop jerry cans filled with water from high altitude but they fell wide of the mark and landed in the marshes. Some landed in the river.

By 1500 hours, the water problem was acute. The dryness caused peculiar effects. One result was that men's tongues began to swell tremendously, almost completely filling the cavities of their mouths, preventing them from speaking coherently. Hardin commandeered what little water was left and kept it for the radio operator. One man had to be understandable on the radio.

Phelps ordered the men not to drink the river water. It was contaminated with everything from hookworms to typhoid. Some ignored his order.

The air force continued its bombing and gunships added their power. The company didn't know that two other companies had been airlifted behind the Viet Cong positions and were slowly making their way towards them. Another two companies were to the west, fighting their way through mosquito-filled swamps at a snail's pace that infuriated the brigade commander. A tight web was closing in on the Viet Cong, but it was taking a long, long time.

The sun baked them relentlessly, steam rising slowly from the river bank that never seemed to dry. They felt abandoned and were becoming quarrelsome among themselves. Phelps feared a mutiny but had no idea what he would do if it came. He hoped Hardin could keep the men under control. They opened all the C-ration cans and drank the fluids inside, including the preservatives. The fruit juice gave them life but the sugar in it made them even more thirsty.

Darkness fell, the river rose on schedule and they spent a second night as before. The number of mosquitoes seemed to double almost as if the insects sensed a weakened prey. Men crawled into the marsh looking for the lost water cans but could not find them.

The next day brought the sounds of distant battle as the other companies finally began to close with the enemy. There was no relief, no resupply. Two wounded men had died during the night, another would not live long.

They drank their own piss and tried squeezing water from the mud by twisting it in pieces of cloth. The result was as black as the river. Their lips cracked and they tried to soothe the pain with mud. Four men collapsed with heat exhaustion and Wop had no saline solution to give them.

The sounds of battle grew closer and more intense. They realized that they were only part of something much bigger, but the feeling of abandonment did not let up one bit. They could not speak to one another but only grunted. They had little energy and lay motionless, oblivious to the command helicopters that flew back and forth over their position. Radio calls came demanding situation reports, but no one bothered to answer.

During the third night, two men disappeared. No one ever learned what had become of them. Jap later guessed they had tried to desert by swimming the river but were too weak.

On the fourth day, Lieutenant Phelps died. It happened incredibly fast. He just lay back and died. Heat exhaustion works that way.

The men stopped sweating. They had very little body fluid left. No one was shooting at the Viet Cong but the enemy continued to fire at anyone who moved.

Boyd found it hard to focus his thoughts on anything. A sense of madness had started to take over his brain. It was hard to breath because his tongue almost completely filled his mouth. In desperation, several men cut their tongues with their knives. It reduced the swelling very little and only added to the pain of their cracked skin.

A hum developed in Boyd's ears like a motor running. He could see clearly-the world was covered by a thin veil.

They hardly heard the final battle. The Viet Cong were forced from their bunkers and destroyed. A few were able to slip away finding a tiny space between the American units. Bravo Company didn't even know it was over until the first supply ships landed. The chopper crews were baffled when no one rose to unload the food, water and ammunition they had brought. The crewmen had to do it, then radioed that something was dreadfully wrong.

A relief platoon was landed by helicopter and reported that they needed a huge medevac. The platoon medic could not find ten men able to stand.

They flew them out in Chinooks, twenty

at a time. The hospital at Dong Tam was overwhelmed, so they flew them all the way on Long Binh where doctors exclaimed they had never seen so many dehydration cases at once. They put thermometers in their rectums, gave them saline fluid by IV and flooded their bodies with cool water to lower their temperatures. One man had a temperature of 109 before he died.

The after-action report was glowing in its terms. More than 500 Viet Cong had been killed. American losses stood at 58 killed, 120 wounded. There was considerable mention of the heroic "holding action" by Bravo Company. The brigade commander was decorated and sent back to the states to the Army War College. Lieutenant Phelps and Dancer received Bronze Stars-posthumously. A doctor at Long Binh wrote an official report protesting the terrible suffering of the soldiers and loss of life from lack of water. He was reprimanded and his report shredded. Sergeant Hardin received a Silver Star. Boyd received a Bronze Star for his rescue of the radio operator in the previous battle. An aging general, who walked with a pained slowness, accompanied by a nervous doctor and a bored-looking general's aide holding a box of medals, pinned it to his pillow.

"Congratulations, soldier. You men won a great victory,' the general said. He sounded very insincere.

Boyd thought a moment about the greatness of nearly dying of thirst and of Dancer bleeding to death because there was no relief, no medevac.

"General, if we won a victory, I hope we never lose," Boyd replied through swollen, cracked lips, then turned his head away. When he was discharged from the hospital, he left the medal on the pillow. As he left the ward, he noted that all the other men had done the same.

In dribbles and drabs the men of Bravo Company were released from the hospital and driven back to Camp Bearcat. Boyd and Youngblade found themselves in the back of the same deuce-and-half truck. They were still weak and dispirited and were told the company would stand down for another four days at least. Within hours, most of them were very drunk, having bought all the booze their ration cards would allow. The liquor burned their lips but they compensated by just pouring it into their mouths. Boyd had considerable trouble finding his rucksack and diary. He was so far behind in making entries that he skipped several pages and made a single notation.

Day 321. Have returned to Bearcat. Was surprised at the changes. The headquarters and officers are getting Adams Huts built for them. These are pre-fab aluminum buildings on cement bases. Some are air-conditioned. There is a rumor that a swimming pool is going to be built here. Can't believe that's true. Nothing is too good for our Base Camp Warriors. Two men in fourth platoon got into a fight with the military police. The MP's tried to turn them away from the PX because their uniforms were so scruffy. They're in the stockade. The poop is that they like it there better than being in the field. Chickenshit seems to be coming to Vietnam. We're supposed to get 9th Infantry shoulder insignia sewed on our combat fatigues. So far no one has done it. Youngblade, Jap and The Pope are back. No one knows where Olive Oyl is. He was released from the hospital but disappeared. He's listed as AWOL right now. Where the hell would you go in this country? Kuhn hasn't come back. If he's lucky they'll send him to Japan. Don't know if a missing finger is worth a ticket home. If so, a lot of guys are going to shoot their fingers off.

Helped Jap box up Dancer's stuff to send home. Not much to send really. The collection agencies aren't going to get their money. Something wrong with my guts. I'm shitting all the time. Knowles has the shakes or something. He's acting real strange. He's drinking non-stop and won't talk to anyone. The Bible which The Pope gave me disappeared in the hospital. Maybe I'll ask him for another. Maybe I won't bother him. I haven't seen him reading his. Hardin is beating on everyone for no reason. He thinks Wop is stealing morphine and using it on himself. I went to the supply section for a new M-16 and the sergeant gave it to me no questions asked. Thought for sure I'd have to sign my life away for a lost weapon but he didn't say a word. I hope we never go back to the Delta. Truth is, we can't fight there. No one can. Received four letters from my mother. Wrote her a short note on the back of the lid of a C-ration box. If you don't send something home, the Red Cross comes looking for you. They showed a movie in the mess hall, "Revolt on Sunset Strip" with Aldo Ray. Ultimate bad flick, everyone left before it was over. Got drunk on rum and coke in my hootch with Moore. I think he's mental or suicidal or something. Says he was wounded four times when he was with the 25th. I have lost all confidence in our generals. I don't think they have any idea of what happens on the battlefield. Too hot to sleep. Rumor is we're going to get an easy operation next week-guarding convoys to and from Vung Tau. Hope it's true.

Chapter 3
WAR ZONE C

DAY 317. I could be a great base camp warrior. We spend most of our time drinking, sleeping and bullshitting. We're supposed to be doing maintenance on our tracks but we just pretend to do it. Hell, Chrysler built those things to last. They don't need maintenance. We just clean them up a bit and make it look like we did the servicing. Some of the guys drove them to the "car wash" out on Highway 1. It's really a whore house where little kids wash vehicles while their mama sans screw the drivers. It's hard to believe the changes since we were here last. The engineers are paving everything that doesn't move. They're bringing in air-conditioned house trailers for colonels and generals. A regiment of Thai soldiers took over the northern end of the camp. They're called the Queen's Cobras. They're sup-

posed to be good jungle fighters. We're "second reserve" which means its unlikely we'll do squat unless something big goes down. We have a new company commander and a new brown bar platoon leader. Both just from the states. The lieutenant wanted to give The Pope an Article 15. He told The Pope to go on Shit Detail and burn the diesel drums under the latrines. The Pope refused. He said only the REMF do that. The company commander supported The Pope. He seems like a regular sort. No one knows where the hell Olive Oyl is. Hardin is fit to be tied about that. Jap went to see Kuhn in the hospital at Long Binh. Kuhn is smacking his hand against the bed frame at night so it won't heal. Jap went over to the NCO club to get drunk and see a floor show. He got kicked out because he was wearing jungle fatigues. The manager said you can't come in unless you're wearing a sports shirt. Isn't there a war going on or something? Some men are having a soft time of it over here. They have no idea what is happening beyond their base camps, air conditioned hootches and bars.

The men of Bravo Company hoped that Division Headquarters had forgotten about them. With each passing day, they became more slack, much to the annoyance of their new company commander, Captain Semple. He was a National Guard officer who volunteered for Vietnam. He was also the Assistant Attorney General of Kansas who said he wanted to be governor some day and combat service would look great on his resume. He was a somewhat overweight, balding man who meekly implored the platoon sergeants to "tighten up." Helmets had been discarded in favor of soft hats, and the men seemed to be doing nothing but wandering from hootch to hootch, drinking and listening to loud music. Sergeant Hardin assured the new commander that the men would snap to when they were needed.

Lieutenant Aaron was an R.O.T.C. graduate who tried to assert his authority by giving endless orders which were generally ignored. He stomped around constantly muttering, "We gotta get some discipline around here."

Nor were all the distractions invented by the soldiers. After a tedious inspection of the outer defenses of the camp, the Division Operations Officer noted that the cleared area between the berms and the barbed wire around the camp looked like a race track. From this tiny germ of an idea came the grand scheme for the army's first tank races.

Each unit was permitted to enter one Sheridan tank in the race. The course was to be twice around the perimeter of the camp. The only rule was no shooting at each other.

The mechanics worked feverishly, stripping every piece of unnecessary equipment from their tanks, tuning the engines and making certain the tracks and drive wheels were adjusted. The wagering was in the thousands of dollars and instant bookies appeared everywhere. The odds-on-favorite was the 3-5th Cavalry. They had a driver from hell and their mechanics had adjusted the engine to take aviation fuel.

At 1600 hours on the scheduled day, thousands of men lined the berms around the camp. If the Viet Cong had any inkling of the event, they could have caused enormous casualties with a few rockets. The five tanks lined up abreast at the starting line, each marked by a different colored pennant. The division commander was the official starter and decided to use a 105 mm howitzer. When he pulled the lanyard, there was a mighty cheer and a huge cloud of dust as the drivers tried to "lay steel."

As the odds makers had predicted, the 3-5th had a hot vehicle that quickly pulled away from the others, its yellow pennant bent back and its dust making it hard for the other drivers to see.

When they reached the first corner, the absence of rules gave the tank on the inside a considerable advantage. He pulled hard to his right and smashed into the left side of another tank, which in turn lurched into a third. This tank lost a track, which flailed and flapped dangerously as it came apart. At high speed the driver could not steer and roared straight ahead, through the barbed wire and into the mine field beyond.

Hundreds of voices cheered as the tank sped straight into the mine field, setting off dozens of anti-personnel mines like fire crackers. Everyone laughed except the engineers whose job it would be to replace them all. The driver eventually walked back, being careful to stay in the tread marks lest he find an unexploded mine.

On the second corner, a tank from an armored brigade couldn't negotiate the turn and flipped over. There was something of a stunned silence as the driver crawled out of the wreck.

"You can't roll a tank, can you?" an incredulous old warrant officer asked a group of tankers.

"No," several men agreed. "You can't."

It would have been no contest if the 3-5th driver had just cruised to an easy victory. Instead, he wanted to see just how fast his tank could go. As he entered the home stretch, he gave it all he could and blew the motor out of it. The high octane fuel had collected in unburned drops in the exhaust until it exploded back into the engine. Unfortunately for the tank close behind him, it was hard to see that the 3-5th's tank had suddenly stopped. He clipped it, tearing a track off in the process. The driver tried to continue with one track but simply drove in a circle.

The men who had bet on the tank with the blue pennant were ecstatic. All their driver had to do was coast across the finish line. Indeed he tried, but less than one hundred yards from victory his engine simply died. The tank slowed, then stopped, and refused to start again.

Several minutes went by as confusion reigned about the outcome. Loud and vocal arguments erupted as to whether the blue tank should be declared the winner because it was the closest to the finish line but the division commander declared the race a draw and all bets canceled.

The troopers of the 3-5th, bereft of their potential profits, set out to beat their driver to a pulp while the engineers pondered how they would get the other tank out of the mine field. The division headquarters staff went off to the officers' club for an all-night Happy Hour. Everyone generally agreed that it had been an outstanding race and that it should be a regular event.

By 1900 hours Boyd and Moore were in their hootch and were extremely drunk. Moore had introduced Boyd to the joys of Jack Daniels but had then strangely switched to making Black Russians. Boyd rejected them as sickenly sweet. They also made Moore visit the piss tube outside the hootch every twenty minutes.

The stale air hung oppressively beneath the canvas tent that covered the make-shift wooden building. They talked end-lessly about food, their favorite restaurants and recipes.

By 2100 hours they had run out of booze and set out to find some more. They were successful when they fell through the screen door of Jap's hootch and found that he had passed out without finishing a bottle of vodka. They gratuitously offered to do it for him. There was a small inter-

ruption when Moore spied an enormous
spider in one corner and shot it with a
small .32 pistol he carried. Drunk as he
was, he hit the target dead on. There was
nothing but a black hole through the floor
where the spider had been.

"Nice shot," Boyd politely acknowledged
as he took a swig of vodka. The loud report brought two military police running
and Boyd sent them on a wild goose chase.

"Came from down there," he muttered,
waving his arm in the direction of the helicopter pad.

"Yep. Came from that-a-way," Moore
said as he leaned against the center pole
of the hootch and drained another two fingers from the bottle.

"Whaddya shooting at?" Jap mumbled
from his cot, without opening his eyes.

"You, you dumb chink," Moore replied.
"Can't hit you 'cause you keep moving."

By midnight, in the whole of the company, there were only two sober men. One
was the chaplain's assistant, a neurotic
little man who ghosted around, picked up
the unit mail every day and typed letters
for the adjutant. He was also the permanent CQ (Charge of Quarters) every night.
The other was a squad leader who, as a
Mormon, had sworn never to touch the

evil brew. But even they were unaware the Viet Cong had overrun a provincial capital. The company was too drunk to notice the helicopters airlifting the 2-39th infantry out of Bearcat. No one got the message that the 2-47th was now first reserve. Besides, there had never been an occasion when two battalions had to be called up to throw a few guerrillas out of some oversized hamlet.

At 0300 Sergeant Hardin staggered from his hootch to the piss tube, thought about barfing in it, then decided he would ride it out. It was there that a confused and extremely nervous chaplain's assistant, waving a flashlight, found him.

"There's a major at brigade headquarters saying something about the company getting ready to go out," the private stammered.

"Tell him to take a flying fuck at da moon," Hardin replied. "We're stood down to second reserve."

"No," the soldier persisted. "The 2-39th went out hours ago. We're supposed to be at the helipad in thirty minutes to reinforce them. There's a big brew-up in the Delta near Old French Fort."

"Bullshit. Dis company ain't going nowhere, no how," Hardin muttered and started back to his hootch. "At least, I ain't."

"What should I tell him?" the CQ asked.

"Tell him what I said about da moon," Hardin insisted. "Be a good experience for him."

Hardin's idea was not well-received. Within ten minutes, a slew of battalion officers and NCO's roared into the company's compound and verbally trashed Captain Semple and Sergeant Hardin for the condition of the troops and the blatant insubordination of not mobilizing when ordered. The extremely hot air had a somewhat sobering effect upon the company leadership, who, in turn, tried to rouse their platoon sergeants to action. It was one of the low points in military history. Hardin could find fewer than a dozen men who were at all functional. They were supposed to march to the helipad but he ordered trucks instead.

There was no time to brew strong coffee and it would have had an improbable effect anyway. They lifted men up, poured cold water on them and shouted orders. Most of second platoon could not be found at all.

They piled the troops on trucks like cordwood, threw their weapons and rucksacks on after them and hoped for the best. Boyd crawled on to a truck as best he could and pulled Moore up after him. Neither man had his helmet and Boyd had only one magazine of ammunition.

Jap seemed to sober up quickly and worked aggressively with Hardin to carry as many men as they could find to the trucks. He was sweating buckets as the alcohol and adrenaline made a foul mixture.

Hardin finally told Captain Semple that he thought he had half the company on the trucks. They decided that was the best they could do. With a clash of gears and much churning of dust, the truck convoy quickly covered the three hundred yards to the helipad where an aviation company sat impatiently waiting, their props turning slowly.

Getting the men off the trucks and into the Hueys was more difficult than arousing them in the first place. Some men climbed in one side of a helicopter and fell out the other. Hardin ordered them to lie on the floor, piling rifles beside them. Several threw up, which outraged the helicopter crews. The senior pilot had a vigorous argument with Semple that he was not taking off with this drunken lot.

Semple and Hardin finally arranged to have one half-sober man on each ship, with firm instructions not to let anyone fall out the door. He even deputized the chaplain's assistant to take charge of a helicopter, much to the soldier's terror.

"But I don't know what to do! I don't even have a weapon," the soldier protested loudly.

"Shut up and get yo' worthless ass on dat chopper!" Hardin shouted as he grabbed the man by the shirt. "And yo' just better make sure no one falls out!"

When the helicopters lifted off, Boyd managed to sit up, even though his head was spinning and his stomach heaving. It was dark inside the ship and it smelled of vomit and maybe urine. He hoped it wasn't his. He was sweating profusely and thought he might get motion sickness. Some of the other men were slowly trying to rouse themselves, muttering and swearing. One soldier whom Boyd didn't recognize started laughing, a silly, childish laugh. Jap told him to stay on the floor until they landed.

It was an interminably long flight. Boyd thought they must be half way across Cambodia when he felt the ship start to bank and go into a slow decline. He was quite surprised when he felt the skids touch the ground. Pilots seldom actually touched down.

They crawled and slid out the doors—a far cry from the proper dash for cover that was expected of them. They had no idea where to go and simply drifted away from the helicopters, often leaving their equipment behind. In small groups, they walked far enough away from the turning props to allow the disgusted pilots to depart.

The first tiny cracks of dawn helped Boyd and Jap find their way to the edge of a well-kept field. They sat down on the bottom row of a set of wooden benches and looked about. They were in a "hollow" surrounded by bleachers with what appeared to be a scoreboard at one end.

Within a few minutes, the entire company was sitting or lying on the wooden benches. Some men moaned and threw up on the grass. In the distance they could hear the sound of sporadic gunfire. It sounded miles away.

A small street ran horizontal to the field and they could hear a motorbike, its tell-tale "braaaaat" noise suggesting it was coming towards them.

"Where the hell are we?" Boyd asked, doubting that anyone had the answer.

"I gotta stop drinking so much," Jap answered, holding his head in his hands. "I'm hallucinating. This looks like a football field."

Boyd could see that Hardin and Semple were looking at a map and discussing their situation with considerable arm waving. Boyd could only catch bits and pieces of their words but it was clear Hardin thought they should go no further since half the men were without weapons or equipment and many were extremely ill.

The motorbike interrupted their debate as it came through a small gate and headed straight across the field towards them. Hardin took the safety off his M-16.

The bike was a tiny Japanese model that made the noise of a Harley. It had a single rider, a small man in his forties dressed in an immaculate white suit complete with a Panama hat. He carefully put his bike on its stand and walked towards the two Americans. He removed his hat, made a small bow and smiled graciously.

"Hello. Please. Hello. I am Mr. Lee," the Vietnamese said, revealing some gold teeth.

"That supposed to mean something?" Hardin asked suspiciously.

"I am stadium manager," the man added, with a certain pride in his voice.

"Where are the Viet Cong?" Semple asked, getting down to more businesslike matters.

"Viet Cong all gone," the man replied confidently, waving his arm in a wide circle. "All gone this morning. There were only two or three of them."

"What was that shooting?" Semple asked.

"Just local militia. I think they sometimes shoot at nothing just to make noise."

"Are there other American soldiers nearby?"

"No. Just you," the man answered.

"Where do you suppose the 2-39th is?" Semple asked Hardin.

"Where are we? Hey, Lee-what the hell is this place?" Hardin asked.

"Football stadium. Americans call it soccer. I am the manager," Mr. Lee explained, bowing again. "I have to prepare for a very important game this morning. Do you wish to see the game? There will be no charge for you."

"There's supposed to be a war on and you are going to have a soccer game?" Semple asked incredulously.

"Oh, yes," Mr. Lee assured him. "A very

important game. Championship game."

"I doan believe dis shit," Hardin sputtered. "They said a town had been overrun. They airlift us into a football field. And now we're gonna watch a game?"

"Maybe we oughta deploy some security," Semple mused aloud.

"Maybe we oughta just go home," Hardin offered in return.

"What! And miss the game?" Jap shouted as loudly as he could without splitting a blood vessel in his head. He started to laugh but a pain behind his eyes stopped him quickly.

"Maybe we should put a couple of men up by that scoreboard," Semple continued. "Just in case."

"Captain, just call battalion and tell dem to come and get us," Hardin insisted.

"I don't know where my radio operator is," Semple replied. "Besides, I'm in a lot of shit now because the company was drunk. If this operation turns into a complete snafu, I can kiss my career goodbye."

"Whaddya gonna do?" Hardin wanted to know.

"Well, we could just hang out here for a while. We could say that we did encounter some Charlies and drove them off. We need an after-action report that says we did something. Y'know?"

"I think I'm gonna like him," Jap said quietly to Boyd.

Under Mr. Lee's efficient direction, the game started at exactly 1000 hours. Hundreds of people filed in and filled the bleachers, eyeing the Americans with considerable surprise and some mirth. There was room for everyone and a holiday spirit evolved. Vietnamese men wore immaculate white shirts with razor sharp creases, and oversized sunglasses. The women had parasols to keep the sun off their heads. Vendors sold cold beer and a funny-tasting sausage to the soldiers who had Vietnamese money in their pockets. The team in green shirts outclassed the team in red shirts. The Americans didn't cheer much because it increased cranial throbbing but the beer helped to ease that. Jap muttered something about taking a hair off the dog that bit you. Even Hardin seemed to relax and get into the spirit. He tried to help the red team until the referee ordered him off the field. When the game was over, the victorious green team ran around the field several times, then ran out the gate. The spectators bid the Americans good-bye in a quick torrent of quacking sounds and left on their motorbikes. The field suddenly seemed deadly silent and the men noted that there was no litter. The Vietnamese didn't throw thrash around their stadiums.

Semple was able to get the choppers back by 1700 hours and they flew back to Bearcat. The 9th Division Old Reliables newspaper printed an exciting Action Report that announced the liberation of another communist-conquered town after a short but fierce battle. Captain Semple received an Army Commendation Medal and everyone was generally happy about that as he seemed like a reasonable fellow.

The stand-down period ended with a flurry of events, including a major buildup of Viet Cong and North Vietnamese along the Cambodian border. It was also highlighted by the return of Olive Oyl, dutifully escorted by two large military policemen. There was much hand-slapping and high-five's all around, with the exception of Sergeant Hardin who thoroughly trashed the errant man behind the mess hall. Olive Oyl didn't seem to mind the beating much, and narrated to an attentive audience where he had been.

"While I was in the hospital, I met this

brother I knew from basic training. He was in the hospital buying sheets from this medical officer who steals them. He took me into Saigon to get some good Cambodian Red, you know? He lives with this whore in Cholon. I couldn't believe what I saw. There are hundreds of GIs living there. They're AWOL. Deserters. They live with whores, steal shit off the docks, black market, have clean beds, hot showers, eat the best food, get stoned on the best dope. They're out of this war, man."

"You mean they just live there all the time?" Jap asked.

"Exactly. There's a whole section of the city that is just theirs. The black brothers have their section; whitey has his. The White Mice-these Vietnamese police in white uniforms-don't mess with them because they're all on the take. The army is afraid to go in there. I moved in with this brother and his woman. Just temporary until I could find a woman and a place of my own. Man, it's a crazy world. There are Chinese drug dealers, Hong Kong whoremongers, Korean big time gamblers-you name it. They got warehouses full of stolen stuff. They got trucks, generators and bulldozers. They just drive it off the docks. I had no intention of coming back here."

"So, what happened?" Boyd asked. He found the whole scenario weird.

"I got careless. Me and another brother stole a jeep in broad daylight and it stalled on us. Shit, man, I coulda painted that and sold it for nine hundred bucks. Military police had my black ass before you could say 'Hey, hey, LBJ.' The Army busted me back to buck private, fined me five hundred dollars and extended my tour sixty days. Don't mean shit cause first chance I get, I am outta here."

"Sergeant Hardin will be watching you," Moore chipped in.

"Yeah, well Old Hard-on will have to have eyes in the back of his head to see me go. And if he becomes too much of a problem, he may have an accident."

Olive Oyl's return was more dramatic than Kuhn's. He strode off a helicopter one afternoon, his hand still in a partial cast. But as the surgeon had left the fingers free to move, he had been pronounced combat fit. He was in a dark mood even before learning that his precious shotgun was lost. He then sunk into a moody abyss.

They convoyed out of Bearcat in the early morning, the recon platoon leaving two hours before the main party. With military police blocking major intersections, they headed north, the tracks making a near-deafening rumble upon the asphalt that had been layered over the red clay of Highway 1. Boyd lay back on the sandbags and tried to get some sleep but the sun soon baked him so thoroughly he abandoned the idea.

For the first time, the men got a close look at Saigon. They drove straight through the heart of the city on their way north, the police trying to clear away the buses, pedicabs and bicycles. The buildings were generally low, no more than two stories high. They were often painted wild colors. The city was a forest of billboards, hawking American cigarettes, movies and Coca Cola. There were street vendors everywhere, selling everything from Tide to combat boots. If black marketing was supposedly illegal, there was no attempt to hide it.

The convoy plodded along for another four hours before leaving the pavement and turning west along a dusty, one-lane road. This became a wide trail, then a path, then disappeared entirely. The tanks were now "breaking bush" as they headed for the Cambodian border.

Overhead, powerful Chinook helicopters came into view, pallets of ammunition and 105-howitzers slung beneath their bellies. Boyd quickly concluded that they were going to build a firebase with an artillery battery.

The position that the brigade commander had chosen was in a small clearing, surrounded by triple-canopy jungle. A combat engineer unit was already there, cutting trees to enlarge the firebase. With chain saws and bulldozers, they were creating a cleared strip a hundred yards wide.

The tanks and tracks were slowed by a tangle of fallen trees and branches yet to be scraped away. They began fanning out towards positions behind earthen mounds the bulldozers had made for them as part of a defensive plan. The men were thirsty and hungry and had hopes of A-rats being flown to them. There was no sense of danger or apprehension. After all, the engineers had been there for hours. Perhaps that's why it was so astonishing when Lieutenant Aaron's track blew up.

Boyd was watching some engineers prepare to blast down a tree with C-4 explosives when he heard the explosion to his immediate front. Youngblade hit the track brakes with a suddenness that nearly threw the entire squad to the ground.

Two vehicles ahead they could see a fireball still unfolding in a cloud of smoke and debris. The outline of the track itself could hardly be seen.

The engineers stopped their work and stood transfixed. The other vehicles sat silent, men unsure whether to dismount or stay where they were. Boyd saw Hardin dash past his track, a fire extinguisher in his hand. He stopped, then ordered everyone to get away.

There was nothing to be done. The vehicle was an inferno of burning fuel and exploding ammunition. They dismounted and took cover behind their vehicles as boxes of machine gun ammunition exploded, sending bullets in every direction. The Chinooks had still not completed the drop of the howitzers and ammunition when bullets began punching holes through their sides. The pilots quickly released the slings and let their loads crash to the ground. Two of the guns were hopelessly damaged.

It burned for three hours, the fire so hot some of the aluminum walls of the track melted. When it died down and they could get close enough with fire extinguishers to put it out, all that remained was a smoking black hulk. Of the five men

who had been on the vehicle, only one survived. He had been blown off the vehicle,
landing some fifty feet to the right. Other
than a broken arm and shrapnel in his
neck, he had miraculously survived. Lieutenant Aaron had been standing in the
hatch directly over where the explosion
had come through the floor. They found
only fragments of his body. He had been
in Vietnam just short of two weeks. The
machine gunner and squad leader had
been blown to pieces. The charred skel-
eton of the driver was stuck so tightly to
the melted frame of his seat, they had to
remove the seat with him. Four men volunteered to do it but two became ill and
gave up the task. Wop and another medic
from the artillery batter managed to do it.

"You're supposed to have cleared this
area!" an enraged Captain Semple shouted
at the first-lieutenant in charge of the engineers.

"We did!" the officer protested. "We went
over the whole area with mine detectors.
We've been driving all over this place our-
selves. I don't know how we could have
missed that."

"If I lose another man because of your
incompetence, I'll tie you to a track and
use you as a mine sweeper," Semple promised.

The engineers dragged the shattered remains of the vehicle away and studied the crater and the floor of the track. No ordinary mine could have done so much damage. They concluded it had been an unexploded American artillery shell buried in the ground, with the detonator screwed into the nose.

Semple and Hardin, sensing that their men had been greatly unnerved by the huge bobby-trap, tried to keep everyone busy. But every time they looked at the burned track, their thoughts flooded back to their vulnerability and how the prospect of sudden death was always there.

Suddenly every man seemed to have developed deep-set, "hurt eyes." They looked like frightened or angry animals. They moved in sudden jerks and erratic ways.

"Goddam country. Goddam people. Goddam army. Goddam mines," Kuhn kept muttering as he kept trying to fill a sandbag with his one good hand. He didn't seem to care that nothing was going in the bag.

Moore moved to help Kuhn, then suddenly stood up straight and said in a slow, steady manner what they all felt: "It's payback time, brothers. The first dink that gets in my way..."

Boyd worked with Knowles filling sandbags. The man said nothing and didn't answer anything Boyd asked. He was sweating terribly and his hands seemed shaky.
After an hour, he suddenly asked Boyd to
go with him to the latrine. It seemed a most
unusual request.

"I just want to be where no one can
overhear us," Knowles said as he went
through the motions of using the facility.

"You certainly pick your spots," Boyd
replied.

"Did you see that?"

"See what?"

"What happened to those men? To the
L.T. and the others?" Knowles said.

"Yeah, I saw it," Boyd replied. "Everyone did."

"They were fucking cremated, man,"
Knowles added, his voice cracking slightly.

"I know. What are you trying to say?"
Boyd asked impatiently.

"We're all going to end up like that. All
of us. You, me, Jap, everyone. And for
what? For this lousy country? For these
stinking people? Who cares about them?
I don't. I care about me. I care about my
wife and baby."

Their conversation was interrupted

briefly while Boyd curtly told another soldier waiting to use the latrine to go somewhere else.

"That's understandable," Boyd said. "We all feel that way. We're all counting the days."

"Not me. Not any longer. I'm not gonna die for this shit, whatever it is. I'm outta here," Knowles said firmly. "If I stay here, I'm never gonna see my wife and child. I know it! Do you think the people back home give a shit about us? The draft-dodgers? The politicians? The hippies, pinkos and protesters? We're the dummies. We fight this war while other people get rich and live the good life. They get up each morning, go to work, come home, cut the grass, watch some T.V. and say what a terrible war it is."

"Well, brother, there ain't diddly shit you can do about it. None of us can, except put in our time and count the days."

"You're wrong. There is a way out," Knowles insisted. "And you're it."

"What the hell does that mean?" Boyd asked. He felt very uncomfortable with the whole direction of the conversation.

"I have an AK-47," Knowles explained. "I picked it up at that ARVN camp. I've kept it out of sight. It's my ticket out of here."

"And just how does that work?"

"It won't be long till someone from our squad is put out on a listening post. We make sure we go together. It'll be dark and no one will see the AK. We report enemy infiltration and start back to our lines. Then we fake a fire fight. I'll fire my M-16 at some imaginary dinks and then you fire the AK towards our perimeter. Throw a grenade, maybe. Finally, you put a bullet into my leg with the AK. A nice clean wound, man, but bad enough for me to go home. Not a flesh wound. You have to hit the bone, you know?"

"Are you serious?" Boyd asked incredulously.

"Do I should like I'm fucking joking? You have to do this for me, man. I can't take this shit no more. My nerves are shot. I'm not gonna die for this shit."

"I can't do it," Boyd protested.

"Why not? It's nothing to you. I'd do it for you. Do it for my wife and baby. I've been here long enough. I've done my share of this. Vietnam is a death sentence, man. I've seen a lot of guys get wasted. I'm not going back in a bag. I'm not going back in a match box like those guys who just got fried."

"Get someone else," Boyd insisted.

"I can't trust anyone else. I trust you," came the reply.

"What if it isn't a clean wound and you end up crippled or something?"

"That's better than dead," Knowles hissed. "I'd take that any day. Will you do it? I gotta know."

"Why not just shoot yourself?" Boyd asked.

"It won't look genuine. I want the bullet to come from the rear," Knowles explains. "No one can question that."

Boyd lapsed into silence a moment, not looking at his friend's imploring face. The plan wasn't that difficult and Knowles had done more than his share of the fighting. He had a mental picture of Knowles bursting from the tree line, his M-60 pouring out the cover fire that may have saved his life. He probably owed the man just what he asked.

"Are you sure?" was all he could ask.

"Never been surer."

"I'll do it. But I hope you never regret it."

"I won't and I'll never forget you doing this. I'm gonna name my next kid after you," Knowles answered. It was the first time he had smiled in weeks. It seemed that an enormous weight had been lifted from his spirit.

The two men waited for their opportunity but it seemed infuriatingly slow in coming. Long before they were selected for a listening post, their platoon was sent on a sweep of a long-abandoned hamlet, overgrown with jungle and pock-marked with shell craters. As the senior NCO, Jap was temporary platoon leader. They walked for half a day, slashing away the jungle growth and vines with machetes. Jungle was not what Boyd thought it would be. He had imagined a rain forest like in the Tarzan movies. Instead, it was a dark, dank impenetrable wall of green. Men got caught on just about everything and had to be cut loose by their buddies. They had great trouble keeping track of each other. A man only ten feet away could vanish into the foliage. The air was humid and lifeless and the men sweat profusely as they hacked their way to their objective. They were told it was a Viet Cong supply base but all they found were collapsed huts and crude bomb shelters. A short distance away, they stumbled upon a peculiar configuration in an open area. It was a collection of low walls constructed of mud and bricks. The walls seemed to be laid out in little squares. They approached it with great caution. Almost simultaneously, they realized what it was.

Artillery shells and bombs had heaved up much of the earth in the clearing, tossing about pieces of wood and human skeletons and rotting bodies.

"Christ, it's a cemetery," Jap said, wrinkling up his nose in disgust at the smashed human remains.

"Even the dead don't get any peace in this lousy country," Moore added as he kicked at a skull perched at the edge of a bomb crater, seemingly mocking him. "Man, you kill a dink and he won't stay dead."

The area reeked of gas leeching from rotting human remains and from the earth itself.

"Let's get outta here," Boyd said to Jap. "I can't stand this."

"Right after we check that building," the squad leader insisted.

Near the center of the cemetery was a small building, or what remained of it. It had been well-constructed, with painted walls and an elaborate roof. There were no windows, just portico-like openings. They stepped through the openings carefully, fearful of booby-traps. There was debris ev-erywhere and most of the roof had collapsed. What remained seemed like a little store, with narrow shelves along the walls. Clay pots and small clay statues were broken and scattered about.

"It's a shrine," Jap declared. "A shrine for their ancestors."

Curiosity replaced caution somewhat and the soldiers poked and pried among the ruins, wondering who had lived and died here and what these artifacts meant.

Youngblade stood in the middle of the building and stared up through a gaping hole in the roof. Then he made a single pronouncement.

"Don't touch anything. We're not wanted here," he said very solemnly, then left.

The others looked at each other a moment, then laughed.

"The Great Spirit is spooking the Injun," Moore laughed.

They rummaged about for another ten minutes, then, finding nothing of value, one by one left the building and the spirits of the dead alone. Only Knowles found something worth taking. He showed Boyd a little carving about the size of his thumb that looked like a fat man holding a bowl.

"I think it's ivory," he said. "A piece is

broken off but the rest might still be worth something."

"I think you should put it back," Boyd suggested.

"No, I'm gonna keep it. Might bring me luck," Knowles insisted, tucking it in his shirt pocket and giving it a little tap. "Might bring me that million dollar wound."

They spent a miserable night a hundred yards from the village. They didn't dig foxholes but just fanned out in the dense jungle and became a meal for mosquitoes that seemed impervious to their repellent. It was one of the longest nights Boyd had ever known.

At morning light, they were soaking wet with dew. They ate cold C-rats and started the endless process of fighting their way through the green sea that surrounded them. Jap received orders to continue west towards the Cambodian border. Resupply would be that night by air.

Youngblade took the point, moving a few feet at a time, then stopping to listen. And smell. He always said that he could smell Vietnamese better than he could hear them. The rest of the platoon was strung out behind him in a long, snaking column. When he found what appeared to be an old trail that was partly grown over, he elected to follow it. Trails lead to some place important. It was easier traveling. It was a mistake.

Youngblade would have seen a wire strung across the trail if there had been one. He would have spotted a Claymore in the trees. He would have sensed the presence of a sniper. He knew just about every booby-trap ever invented. Except the one that killed him.

The men hit the ground as a powerful explosion rocked the jungle, throwing dirt and bits of wood into the air. They gripped their weapons and one man fired off a nervous burst before Jap ordered him to stop.

Youngblade had died instantly, the potent blast indicating a big mine or buried shell. It took twenty minutes to get what was left of his body out of a tree. They did not look for his missing right leg. The Pope and Kuhn bagged and tagged their friend without exchanging a single word. Out of the corner of his eye, Boyd could see Knowles watching them. The man's eyes were black holes in a dead face. Boyd avoided eye contact. He knew what Knowles was thinking.

Moore poked and sniffed around where the mine had been buried. He collected a piece of blue wire, the burned remains of a Japanese flashlight battery and a piece of wood with a metal strip attached.

"I've seen this before," he said solemnly as he showed the parts to the others. "They bury the mine with a battery-activated detonator. They split a stick of wood and put a strip of metal on each half, then pack mud between the strips. When a man steps on the stick, his weight forces out the mud, the two pieces of metal touch and complete the circuit, and the mine goes off."

The squad members passed the bits and pieces among themselves and realized how vulnerable they were to instant death from such devices. They looked around at the placid, quiet jungle. The jungle they had come to hate. Dark, stinking, endless, menacing and concealing death at every turn. They felt angry and frustrated but there was no enemy to take it out on.

In view of his experience, Jap asked Moore to take the point. Boyd was second in the file, Knowles behind him. He nervously tapped the little statue in his pocket and muttered something about being too short to die now.

With Moore in the lead, they abandoned

the trail and moved through the jungle, walking parallel to it. Their progress was so slow it became little more than a crawl. Moore stopped after every five steps and crouched down. Boyd followed suit. They listened, sniffed the air, then moved on.

It was mid-afternoon when they heard the voices. Moore suddenly froze and raised his right hand. There was silence and for a moment he thought his mind was playing tricks on him. Voices again. This time they all heard them. Quacking, singing voices.

The men moved quickly into a defensive position, facing left and right. Moore inched forward slowly, studying the ground before putting down each foot softly. It took him ten minutes to reach the edge of a small clearing. Boyd and Knowles quietly moved up beside him. They pushed back some branches and were startled to realize how close they were to the source of the sounds.

The clearing had been made by a large bomb. It had also blown out a crater that had collected water. There were four naked Viet Cong bathing in the little pond, their weapons and uniforms piled at the edge. They were oblivious to the danger and Moore saw no one posted as security.

The Vietnamese were chattering and laughing, wrestling, splashing water and pushing each other like school boys playing hooky. Boyd was taken aback by the sight. They were scrawny, little people who didn't look like they were more than twelve years old.

Using quick sign language, Moore made the plan. Boyd and Knowles split right and left, being careful not to step on any sticks. They removed their helmets so branches could not make any rasping sounds. They could still see Moore's vague outline in the jungle. He gave the signal.

Three hand grenades rolled simultaneously over the lip of the crater. There were shouts as the Viet Cong saw the dark objects rolling down the inside bank. Three tried to quickly climb up the far bank. The fourth ducked under the water. The grenades exploded almost in perfect unison, flinging their deadly pieces of hot steel into flesh. The three Americans jumped forward and opened fire on full automatic.

It was over in seconds. The three Viet Cong were scattered around the crater is if they had been laid out in a three-point formation. The fourth half-floated in the water, only part of his face exposed. Most of the top of his head was missing.

As they moved forward to seize the weapons, Boyd saw movement to his right. He whirled and nearly collided with another Viet Cong who was trying to reach a weapon partly hidden from view by the jungle. The guerrillas had posted security! But the man had gone off to relieve himself, leaving his comrades exposed.

Boyd was practically in the man's face-an astonished face, full of fear. They both shouted unintelligible noises, then Boyd smashed the Vietnamese in the head with the butt of his rifle.

The man crashed to the ground, then made a half-roll and tried to scramble into the bush. Boyd leaped after him and hit the guerrilla in the middle of the back. He heard the air go out of the man but he somehow got to his feet and lunged another few feet.

Boyd swore in garbled, single syllables. He was in a fury. He grasped his rifle by the barrel and swung it like an axe, hitting the man in the back of the head this time. He was going to swing again when Moore pushed past him and landed on the Viet Cong in a flying tackle. Jap was suddenly at his elbow, telling him to calm down.

"Gotya, you little son-of-a-bitch!" Moore

shouted as he grabbed the Viet Cong by the hair and pulled him up until he was on his knees. The man was obviously stunned by the blows to his head and offered no resistance.

"Keep your eyes open, damit!" Jap shouted at the rest of the platoon. "There may be more of them."

"Well, lookie here, brothers. We got us a PEE OH DOUBLE U," Olive Oyl said, grinning and poking the man in the ribs with the barrel of his M-16. "How 'bout we have us some target practice?"

"Can that crap," Jap said sharply. "We ain't shooting prisoners. Headquarters wants prisoners."

"Well then, let headquarters get their own prisoners," Kuhn argued.

"Let's ask Boyd. It's his prisoner," Olive Oyl suggested. "Brother, what you wanna do with your prisoner?"

Things had happened so fast, Boyd had no chance to think about it. He had only acted out his reflexes.

"I dunno. Take him in, I guess," he mumbled.

"Beeeep. Wrong answer. Try again, Boyd," Olive Oyl continued, an exaggerated smile on his face. "But you can still win a consolation prize."

"We're taking him with us," Jap insisted loudly. "Collect those other weapons."

None of the men moved and Jap could feel the tension.

"You forgetting Youngblade?" Olive Oyl asked, gesturing with his thumb. "He's right back there in a bag in case you need reminding. Or, should I say, part of him is in the bag." The men had formed a loose circle, with Jap and Olive Oyl squared off inside that circle.

"No, I haven't forgotten," Jap replied, facing the man squarely. "But I'm giving you a direct order not to harm that prisoner."

"Yeah, Jap, you giving the orders. You the acting platoon leader and all that shit but I think this is something we should put to a vote. How 'bout that, brothers?"

Jap and Olive Oyl fell silent, their eyes searching the faces of the others.

The Pope spoke first: "A prisoner is just baggage. We run into more V.C., he'll give us away."

"I say it's pay back time," Moore added.

"Waste the fucker and be done with it," was Knowles's answer. "He's probably the little shit who planted that mine."

No one else spoke.

"Boyd?" Jap asked.

"I don't care," he answered quickly. "Whatever you decide."

"Anyone else?" Jap asked.

A few men shrugged.

"You wanna vote?" Jap asked.

"We did!" Olive Oyl answered sharply. "Majority rules. And majority said waste his ass."

"Anybody say no?" Jap asked quietly.

Silence.

"So, who wants to do it?" Jap asked.

"We all do it," Olive Oyl answered, grasping his M-16 tightly. "That way, no one is gonna rat on nobody because we're all in it together."

The others nodded. There would be no official retribution.

Olive Oyl dragged the Viet Cong to the top of the bank of the crater and sat him upright. The man still seemed dazed and confused about what was taking place. As a parting gesture, Olive Oyl balanced a C-ration can on the man's head. The Americans formed a small line forty feet away, their weapons at the ready.

"Each man gets one chance to shoot the can off his little sloped head," Olive Oyl explained. "We all pay five dollars to whoever does it first. Then we blow him away."

Boyd felt a knot in his stomach. Something inside him said not to participate. A human target was beyond war. It was beyond comprehension. But he was part of something and the image of Youngblade's body in the tree was still vivid. Moore said it was pay back time. They were family. Families stick together.

Moore won the five dollars. Then Olive Oyl counted to three and they emptied their magazines into the guerrilla, knocking him backwards over the bank and out of sight.

It was another five days before Boyd was chosen for listening post. The Pope was to go with him but when Knowles offered to take his place, no one thought anything of it.

They were old hats at this task, so no one bothered to brief them. They had a radio, a password to come back through the perimeter, basic weapons, no helmets, one canteen each. And one AK-47 that stayed hidden until they went out under the cover of darkness. When they were a hundred yards from the line of bunkers they hunkered down in a shell hole. The listening post was the ears of the firebase-the early warning line that the

Viet Cong might be trying to infiltrate. It wasn't a job most men relished because in the event of a major attack listening posts were nearly always overrun. Two men might be sacrifices so that others would be warned.

They weren't supposed to talk at all but they broke the rule and whispered in short sentences. Knowles said he hadn't changed his mind and was upbeat about the prospect of hospital and home. He even had an alternative plan. He would shoot Boyd first, perhaps in the leg or foot, then Boyd would shoot him in the leg. If the Viet Cong were aiming low, it was highly probable they would be wounded in the lower extremities.

"We can both go home," Knowles urged. "We'll have a grand old reunion-a big party, just you and me."

"No, we'll do it the way we planned," Boyd said.

"Why? You like it here? You wanna end up dead for some reason?" Knowles asked, the irritation so obvious in his voice. "You think I'm a coward, don't you?"

"No, I understand what you're doing. It's just not for me. Let's get it over with."

Knowles keyed the handset on the radio three times, the signal that meant they had detected enemy forces. The two men stood up, barely visible to one another in the starlight, and set their plan into motion. Knowles threw a hand grenade into the empty darkness, then fired a quick burst with his M-16. Boyd checked the AK for the tenth time to make certain it was on single shot. He fired a single bullet into the back of Knowles' right leg, just above the ankle. He winced as the man fell down from the impact. He switched the weapon to automatic and fired a burst into air over the firebase.

"You okay?" he asked as he helped the wounded man to his feet.

"Never felt better," Knowles said with a little groan. "Drop the AK and let's di-di."

Boyd abandoned the radio and put his arm under Knowles' shoulder. Moving quickly, they hobbled back to the perimeter until a nervous sentry challenged them.

Knowles gave the password in a loud voice and added unnecessarily, "Don't you shoot me, you idiot." His voice nearly cracked into laughter. He was positively high.

What followed was a blur of activity. Wop bandaged Knowles' leg and was puzzled when the man seemed delighted to hear that he had a smashed tibia. Hardin quizzed Boyd on what happened. The questions and answers flew back and forth like a tennis game.

"How many?"

"Dunno. Saw four or five. Maybe more."

"Coming in?"

"Yeah. Looked like sappers. I think they had those bangalore torpedo things. Hard to see in the dark."

"Yo' get any of dem?"

"I think so. They were real close."

When no ground attack followed, Hardin assumed the listening post had broken up the Viet Cong's attack plans. At 0200 hours the helicopter came for Knowles, guided by two strobe lights set up by the artillery battery.

Knowles was awake but fuzzy from the morphine Wop had given him. Before they put the stretcher on the chopper, the other squad members said their good-byes. Boyd was last. He hugged his friend vigorously. The two men clung to each other, without saying anything further. Finally Knowles whispered in his ear.

"Thanks, brother."

Then, he pressed something into Boyd's hand. It was hard and smooth.

"My good luck charm," Knowles said.

"Keep it. It'll bring you luck, too."

The chopper was on the ground for less than a minute, lifted off, made a wide loop over the firebase as it gained altitude, then disappeared into the night. Boyd felt a sense of relief and sadness but he tried to picture the happy scene when Knowles came off the plane and his wife was waiting for him. He also felt very alone. At least Knowles had someone to go home to.

It was around 0430 hours that they learned the helicopter was missing. The flight time to the field hospital was only forty minutes and the helicopter had not arrived. At 0220 hours, another ground unit had heard a brief, confusing report over their radio. Someone had shouted, "Flick on your lights!"

By dawn, they knew the helicopter had crashed. It might have been shot down or it might have simply had a mechanical failure. For three days, two full companies combed the jungle, working a pattern of squares. They searched from the air and on the ground. They fired no artillery anywhere along the probable flight path of the helicopter. They never found any trace of it.

It seemed impossible that the machine and men could just disappear but the eternal jungle had swallowed them. The metal would rust. The corpses would swell, turn black, then split open. Within weeks insects would strip the bodies to bone, vines would cover everything and no one would ever know.

Day 280. Firebase Emily. It is starting to rain. The monsoon season is upon us. It depresses ev-eryone even more than they already are. It is hard to accept what happened to Knowles. Everyone is in pain about him and Younblade. I desperately want to tell someone the whole story but I don't dare. I'd just end up in jail and that won't bring him back. Maybe his luck ran out when he gave me the little statue. I keep making a twist of the old proverb: If a helicopter crashes in the jungle and no one hears, does it make a sound? And does anyone give a shit? Jap left on R and R to Hawaii, to be reunited with his family. A colonel flew out here from division and asked Jap if he would accept a field commission as an officer. The hitch is that he'd have to extend his tour in Vietnam another six months. Jap said No way, Jose. Olive Oyl has deserted again. He got on a supply helicopter, said he had been called back to Bearcat for something, and flew away.

From Bearcat, he just disappeared. Gone back to Saigon, for sure. Hardin is gonna kill him if he ever is caught a second time. I feel responsible for Knowles death, even though it's what he wanted. I keep telling myself that but I still feet guilty. I tried to talk to The Pope in a roundabout way about it but he shrugged me off. There's something going on with him. He doesn't read his Bible at all anymore. He's smoking pot and I never saw him do that. I realize how close I came to death. If I had done what Knowles wanted, we would have both been on that helicopter. Maybe something was protecting me. Maybe that same something is going to get me through this. Hardin is after Wop again about the morphine. Syringes keep disappearing. I've heard that Wop hardly sleeps at all anymore. He sits up all night, listening to tapes through an earphone. Moore has been sick a lot. He shits constantly and thinks he has malaria but the battalion surgeon says it's just from the water. They won't send him to the hospital. We have a new platoon leader. Lieutenant Baxter. He's a little fat guy with big thick glasses. I can't guess where they found him. He doesn't know shit from shoe polish. No one pays any attention to him. I think about the prisoner we killed. I don't

feel bad about it at all and that's what both-
ers me. I fear that I've become so hard, so
ugly inside, that I've lost the ability to feel
anything. And I wonder if I'll ever get it
back.

Chapter 4
THE RAIN PLANET

DAY 274. Firebase Emily. I recall once reading a science fiction short story called "The Rain Planet." It's about astronauts who crash land on a planet where it rains all the time. Eventually they all go insane. Now I understand how that could happen. Everything is turning to mud and water. It rains so hard, it rains up. The ground is so saturated, the water lays on top and then the wind blows it back up under your poncho, piece of plastic or whatever you use to try to keep dry. Dry? I've forgotten what that is. I don't think I will ever be clean again. I borrowed a little shaving mirror from a guy in 3rd platoon. A dink made it out of flattened beer cans and sold it to him for fifty "pee." What a crock of shit Vietnam is. These people don't even know the world is round. I don't know why we're fighting for this country. I can't believe Knowles, Youngblade and Dancer died so people can pound beer cans into mirrors. I can't see myself in the mirror very well but the face I see is eighty years old. My skin is a mass of zits and when I shave they all start bleeding. I have a huge boil on my elbow. Wop cut it out but it won't heal. He didn't use any pain killer at all. He's out of it so much of the time it's a wonder he didn't cut my arm off. I can't talk to him, he makes no sense. He keeps saying shit about seeing people's guts. He won't eat anything but fruit. The artillery battery is driving us insane. They never seem to give it a rest. They got empty brass shell casings piled up to the sky. Word is we're going on a "deep penetration" to the Cambodian border. If Olive Oyl was here, he'd be saying, "Don't look good brothers." I wonder what became of him. Hardin told me to pack up Knowles' personal stuff to send home. I said I couldn't do it. I think Hardin knows. Every time he says something about Knowles, he looks at me like he's saying: "Yo' did it, didn't yo'?" I don't know why I let him talk me into it.

The monsoon came upon them with a vengeance, making it impossible to read a letter, clean a weapon or take a shit without being soaked to the bone. It was a cold, driving rain that penetrated men's souls.

Spirits sunk to new lows, if that was even possible. The troops huddled in small groups, poncho liners over their steel posts, and talked in short, quick sentences about hot showers and clean sheets. Fights and arguments over nothing became common. They strung shelter-halves over their bunkers but the canvas just collected water until it collapsed under the weight. Their foxholes and bunkers filled with water and they gave up bailing as a wasted effort. The artillery gunners placed rows of sandbags behind their howitzers in a vain effort to stop the guns from sliding in the mud every time they recoiled. With each passing day, the task became more impossible and the cursing gunners simply wrestled the heavy pieces back into position after every round. The inaccuracy of the sliding guns was a constant worry.

"Gawdamit, it's slippier than owl shit on a wet log out there," Kuhn said as he slid into the bunker he shared with Boyd. A resupply helicopter had brought mail along with the food and ammunition. Boyd had been trying to get some sleep but no matter how or where he positioned himself water dripped on his face, a torment that grew in intensity by the hour.

"You stupid fucking redneck. Can't you just talk English? Do you have a cute hillbilly saying for goddam everything?" Boyd snarled back.

"Sure, city boy. Got a million of em. Lot of philosophers in my family."

"Your family? Your family is so in-bred you're your own first cousin."

"Well, since you are so lovable today, I am not going to share this with you," Kuhn said as he pulled a parcel from under his poncho.

"What is it, a new supply of grits, hushpuppies and red-eyed gravy or whatever that pig swill is you keep talking about?"

"Oh, don't I wish! No, but this will do."

Kuhn cut away the outer paper and cardboard with his knife, only to find another box inside the first. He cut that away and found a third box.

"Terrific. A shipment of flavored cardboard. Let's get the pot boiling," Boyd said.

"Stand by, old son," Kuhn said confidently. He cut open the third box and dumped out a large quantity of peanuts, still in their brown shells.

Boyd picked up a handful of the nuts,

threw them over his head and laughed.

"Peanuts? Your family sent you a box of peanuts? Tell me, does your family tree have any forks in it at all?"

"Course not. Don't want inferior stock infecting our herd," Kuhn replied. Then he looked at Boyd very seriously. "That's the first time you've laughed in weeks."

The words hit him like a shock wave. Kuhn was right but it was an irritating truth.

"What did they send you?" he asked quietly.

Kuhn pulled two, labelless black bottles from the box and dangled them in front of Boyd's eyes.

"This, my rotten friend. The finest white lightning ever made."

"What? Moonshine?" Boyd asked suspiciously.

"No, we just sell that to the stupid city people. This is blackberry brandy which my Uncle Clarke makes. There is nothing like it. Clarke is a bit of a philosopher, too. And if you had treated my family with respect, I would have let you have some."

"Respect? Of course I respect your family!" Boyd insisted. "Respect? Gawdamighty, I respected 'em at Shiloh. I respected 'em at Gettysburg. I positively genuflect when they walk by."

"What does that mean?" Kuhn asked.

"It's a compliment, trust me. Open the goddam things!"

"Both of them?"

"Certainly. One for you; one for me."

"You may not get any," Kuhn asserted, holding the bottles away from Boyd's outstretched hand. "No respect."

"The South will rise again."

"Not good enough. Try harder."

"God bless Jefferson Davis, Elvis, the Klan and Colonel Saunders."

"Closer."

"Gimmee one of those suckers or I'll kill you in your sleep."

"I thought you'd never say it right," Kuhn said as he passed a bottle to Boyd.

Kuhn had not understated the qualities of the product. With the first swallow, a tiny bonfire sprang up in Boyd's stomach. With the second swallow, it spread across the entire upper regions of his chest through the roof of his mouth into his brain. The liquor was sweet but not overpowering. An aroma like a bouquet of flowers filled the bunker. They each consumed half a bottle without conversation, just a few belches and tiny compliments to the genius of philosopher Uncle Clarke.

"How come you never get any mail?" Kuhn suddenly asked.

Boyd didn't answer for a while. He was totally unprepared for the question.

"No family. I don't have an Uncle Clarke."

"You got a mother."

"Everybody got a mother," came the quick answer. "Cept you, of course."

"No, I mean you used to get letters from you mother. I know you did. So what happened?"

"Nothing."

"No girl friend?" Kuhn persisted.

"No! What are you? The new chaplain? Let it go, will you?"

They drank quietly for a while, the 180-proof alcohol working relentless to free the rust from their brains.

"What happened with Knowles?" Kuhn suddenly asked.

"Whaddya mean, what happened? You know what happened. What's with you today, anyway?"

"Just wondering."

"You know, the first thing Jap told me when I got here was to stop wondering. You should take that advice."

"You shot him, didn't you?" Kuhn asked slowly, taking a long drag from the bottle.

"Who says?" Boyd shot back.

"Nobody. But he asked me to do it. I said no. I figured he'd find someone else."

"Well, you figured wrong. And I only have one nerve left and you're standing on it."

"Jap knows."

"Knows what? Open your ears. I'm talking to you in English. Even a dumb fucking hillbilly can understand some English. A dink shot Knowles. The copper crashed. I'm not telling you that again."

"I'm just glad I don't have to live with it," Kuhn muttered.

"You may not live at all," Boyd replied as he jumped to his feet, the neck of the bottle in his hand. Before he could launch a blow at Kuhn's head, a familiar voice interrupted him.

"You bastards having a party without me?" Jap said as he slid through the opening in the bunker.

"Well, look who was dumb enough to come back to Slopeland. Thought you had enough sense to desert," Kuhn said, his voice betraying a growing degree of drunkenness. "And what the hell happened to you?"

Boyd stepped back to get a better look at Jap's face in the dim light. The left side was swollen and a large bandage covered the right.

"Not much. Got into a fight and thrown in jail. Gimme some of that," the sergeant said, snatching the bottle from Boyd's hand. "Looks like you ain't treating it proper, anyway. You boys actually find something to disagree about?"

"Nothing important," Kuhn insisted. "So how many hippies kicked the shit out of you?"

"Not sure. Pretty drunk at the time. My father had me thrown in jail. Ain't that a pisser?"

"Sorry 'bout that. No big deal. Mine took a shot at me once," Kuhn replied. "What did you do?"

"One of my sisters got engaged and they had this big engagement party. Her fiancee is a complete muscle bound, dickhead-a football player at the university. I overheard him bragging to a buddy of how he was marrying my sister just so he'd get a lower draft number. He also said he'd enrolled in a seminary in Arizona to study for the ministry. That will keep him outta the draft for another three years. Except there ain't no seminary. Some relative of his set up this phony church and seminary. Guys pay their so-called tuition to get a student draft deferral. It's really just a payoff for a piece of paper. They don't even have to attend. They got two dozen guys enrolled in this seminary who actually play professional football."

"Incredible," Boyd said angrily. "Man, the shit that goes down."

"Naturally I clipped him. His buddy caught me with a good one. My brother jumps in on my side. My mother starts screaming and my father smacks me with a metal chair. Just when I was starting to win, too. Then he had me tossed in jail. Good fun all around. No one, except my brother, is talking to me. They wouldn't even pay my bail. They think Mr. Gridiron is God and that I'm totally psycho."

"You are a psycho, little Jap, to take on a football team. So who paid your bail?" Boyd asked.

"Nobody. I told the judge I had to be on the plane back to 'Nam or I'd be AWOL. He said he thought my most immediate departure would be a very good idea and just let me go. Christ, it stinks in here. You don't realize it till you've been away a while."

"Thank you for that bit of timely news. Gimme back my goddam bottle," Boyd answered.

"What the hell is this war doing to us?" Jap asked. "My family was always close. Really close. I worked with my father in his florist business since I was five. I'm the eldest and we were really close. When I went home, everyone treated me like I was a deceased alien. It was terrible... awkward. Like they didn't know how to talk to me anymore. You know? I remember what Moore said about not belonging anymore. He's right."

"Makes infinite sense to me," Boyd replied. "We're just diseased aliens. Remember the infantry motto: E Pluribus Expendable. Here, have another drink."

The next morning they knew that something big was stirring. Hardin and Captain Semple had a hurried conference with the battalion commander at the small helipad, then began dashing about shouting orders. The news trickled down, subject to the usual wild alterations and confusion of the rumor mill. The only clear facts were that a two-man, long-range reconnaissance patrol had been inserted by helicopter the night before and found themselves smack in the middle of a large North Vietnamese unit. The two frightened solders hid in a tree all night and pleaded to be extricated. An attempt was now being made to do that because a B-52 strike would hit the area in less than an hour. The huge bombers were already airborne when they were diverted by radio from a mission over North Vietnam.

"Listen up!" Hardin bellowed at the squad and platoon leaders. "After the bombers hit the area, we're going in by chopper to finish 'em. Look at yo' maps. The dinks are two clicks north of checkpoint Hilda. Dat's only three clicks from here. Looks like they were headed for us when dey were spotted. Squad leader, check yo' people good. These are hard-core NVA, not local villagers."

Neither the Americans nor the NVA heard or saw the bombers gliding silently at 10,000 feet. As the American troops huddled along the helipad in the pouring rain, they felt the ground begin to shake as the first strings of five hundred pound bombs hit the earth. At first it was just a small tremor beneath their feet. Puzzled, they looked at each other for an explanation. The shaking increased and they could feel it in their bones and joints. Then they heard it. A low rumble became a roar and the earth jerked violently, pitching most of them sharply to the ground.

"Jesus!" was all Boyd could think to say as he got to his knees and was knocked down again. He could see the artillery gunners falling, then trying to run to their bunkers. They must not have got the word and thought they were under rocket attack.

The roaring noise grew louder, as if someone had opened the door to a blast furnace. It was already dark but a strange blackness started to blend into the gray drizzle. The soldiers abandoned the idea of standing up and just sat or knelt on the ground as the earthquake continued for another three minutes. Then, as quickly as it started, it stopped.

"What the hell was that?" a man asked loudly. He received no answer.

"Quit grab-assing! On yo' feet!" Hardin shouted as the line of hueys came into view, nearly scraping the tops of the trees.

With a practiced, dutiful precision, the company ducked under the blades and into the waiting machines in less than a minute. Their faces were taunt. It was old hat, except they knew they were up against North Vietnamese regulars this time.

It was the shortest flight Boyd had ever taken. They had hardly left the firebase when the machines were descending again. Hardin had said the enemy was near, but this close?

The pilots were extremely cautious and found it difficult to get low enough to insert the troops. They hovered more than eight feet above the ground, which was a mass of twisted and broken tree stumps and branches. The men swore and hesitated as they saw how far they were expected to jump into the inhospitable terrain below them. Some put their feet on the helicopter's runners and hung on to the floor with their hands before letting go. To their credit, the pilots strained to hold their machines steady in the air and managed not to pitch the men out violently.

Boyd opted to jump, crashing into a tangled mass of broken tree branches that tore most of the skin off his right arm. His problem was increased when Jap landed on his right leg. Moore gave Jap the same treatment.

"Move it! Dis ain't no football game!" Boyd heard Hardin shouting as he untangled himself from the incredibly deep pile of branches and leaves. He glanced around and was stunned by the sight of their landing zone. All around him there were uprooted trees, root balls, tangled branches and piles of earth several feet high. Boyd had never seen hurricane damage but guessed that it must resemble what he was witnessing. It was very hard to see at all and something irritated his eyes. He looked down at the back of his hand. It was still raining but there was so much earth mixed in with the drops of water that the rain had turned to mud.

"What the hell-it's raining mud," he said to Kuhn, who had made the same discovery.

"I said move it, Boyd!" Hardin bellowed as he stormed by, pushing and shouting at men who seemed without direction.

Slowly they shook off their inertia and formed a loose skirmish line. They began working their way north, stumbling and tripping over the immense pile of debris that had once been a dense jungle. Everything was mud-covered, wet and slimy, and the men fell frequently. The darkness was foreboding and the soldiers kept nervous fingers on their triggers. Someone made a comment that it reminded him of the child's game, Pick Up Sticks.

"Sarg!" the point man from fourth squad called out. His voice was cracked and tense.

"What yo' got?" Hardin shouted back.

"Better come see this sarge," the man insisted. It was evident he was going no further.

Hardin worked his way forward, cursing at the endless masses of branches that barred his path. Boyd and Jap followed close behind him. It took five minutes to reach the forward position where Hardin and the point man were squatted behind a smashed tree trunk, staring at something and whispering. Boyd moved forward to see what it was.

At first he could not make any sense out of the object that resembled a demented artist's idea of sculpture. But there was no denying that the thing was the stock and part of the trigger housing of an AK-47. It had been propelled right through the tree and nearly out the other side. More impressively, there was a piece of green shirt stuck to it. Inside the shirt was a hand and arm, the fingers still gripping the stock.

"Do you believe that?" the point man asked Boyd. The man was nervously chewing gum and having trouble swallowing his saliva. Boyd knew him vaguely. The man was an experienced soldier who had seen a lot of action, but he seemed very unnerved by this spectacle.

"I don't know what to believe anymore," Boyd replied.

"Shut up!" Hardin said. "We doan know what's ahead."

Hardin took his binoculars from his rucksack and scanned the ground in front of them. The dark cloud that seemed to surround them refused to reveal much of its secrets. What he could see clearly troubled him. He handed the binoculars to Jap and went back to find Captain Semple.

They took turns looking through the binoculars, trying to focus on anything they could recognize. The smashed trees seemed to stretch forever. Or at least they could see no end to them. The earth seemed heaved up in a pattern of giant groundhog holes.

Hardin returned in ten minutes and gave the order.

"Captain says we check it out. Spread out, keep visual contact with each other."

The first two squads moved cautiously, picking their way through the obstacle course. After fifty yards, Boyd was confronted by a seven-foot hill of fresh earth that seemed very much out of place. He signaled Jap to cover him and worked his way up the side, then jumped over the lip, weapon ready.

The hill was the edge of a huge crater, as large as the excavation for a house. It was more than ten feet deep. Boyd could see radial marks in the earth fanning out from a burned spot in the center. He also saw a smashed pith helmet and a human foot near the top of the opposite side.

There was no way around the crater, so he scrambled down one side and up the other, only to find himself overlooking another crater. To his right and left he could see other men doing the same. Beyond this crater was another and another. Each displayed its grisly human parts and bits of smashed military equipment.

By the time he reached the eighth crater, he was getting tired. It was also difficult to get up and down the sides which were turning to mud. The craters were slowly beginning to fill with rain water.

In the eighth crater, he found three human torsos, minus limbs and heads. By the tenth crater, the number of torsos rose to eleven. The sides of the crater were impaled with rifles, belts of machine gun ammunition and everything a large unit would carry.

Moore took over the point and they crossed six more craters. The number of dead increased with every rim they crossed. The enormity of the death and destruction weighed on them as heavily as the rain that never let up. There was no exuberance, just astonishment at the carnage.

Out of curiosity, Moore went through the shirt pockets of a torso that was half-planted near the rim of a crater. He found some South Vietnamese money, an I.D. card and a photograph of a family of eight.

"Now, back in Hanoi they'll be wondering why old Lee Wong Dong here don't write," he wisecracked, tossing the card down beside the body.

"Are we gonna do this shit forever?" Jap asked Hardin. "There's nothing but craters and dead dinks from here to India."

"We go on till the captain says we stop," Hardin said. "Gawd, the bombers walked it right over dem."

"How many do you think there were?"

"Dunno. Hundreds. Whole regiment. Gawd bless the air force of the U.S. of A. Dey were headed right for us."

They went on for another half-hour. The trek became more and more difficult; the men were tired, muddy and fed up. The grumbling increased to a near chorus. Boyd and Moore found themselves taking a short rest at the top of a crater, staring down at the familiar sight of scattered remains. The Pope lay beside them, the rain running off the lip of his helmet and down his face. He had a peculiar, far-away expression.

"It's started. I really think it's started," The Pope said quietly, talking more to himself than to the others.

"What has?" Boyd asked indifferently.

"Armageddon," came the answer.

"What's that?"

"Don't you know?"

"If I knew, would I ask you?"

"You'll know soon enough then," the soldier said angrily, then slid down the side of the crater and walked away.

"That guy's coming undone," Moore commented. "He's dinky dau-crazier than a shit house rat."

"I never know what's going on with him anymore," Boyd agreed. "But he's no crazier than the rest of us."

"With killing power like this, how come we can't win the goddam war?" Moore asked.

"Because for every one we kill, they got ten more," Boyd suggested. "Dinks are like ants. Somewhere there's a great big old queen dink laying millions of eggs. The eggs hatch into little dinks and they grow up to be big dinks..."

"Shut up," Moore groaned. "I got the point."

They stumbled around for another two hours before the hueys came back for them. It was difficult getting back into the ships. The soldiers balanced themselves on the crater lips as the pilots tried to hover low enough for them to climb in, one at a time. Some men slipped and fell into the craters which were rapidly becoming deep, dangerous pools of muddy water. Their comrades had to pull them out using their rifles as grappling poles. Not a single shot had been fired but the troops felt a great relief to be escaping from this enormous slaughter house. As they lifted off and Boyd looked down at the desolate landscape with its hideous tenants, he thought back about what The Pope had said. He knew all too well what Armageddon meant. He just didn't want to face up to it. The earth didn't even look familiar to him anymore. He was in another world, in another time. The Rain Planet. And he felt it was dragging him down into a pit from which he'd never escape. He touched the little statue in his pocket and thought about Knowles. If I get out of here alive, I'll go see his family, he thought. I'll tell them the truth. But he knew he wouldn't.

Boyd and Jap were cleaning their M-16's when they saw Hardin walking towards them, two other men in tow. Somehow replacements stood out like sore thumbs. It was an overwhelming sense of deja vu. It was one of the few moments when the rain stopped. Boyd wore a brimmed Australian bush hat he had bought from a roadside peddler. Jap wore a red bandanna tied about his head. They shared a bottle of whiskey, a beer and a joint.

"Jap," Hardin began.

"I know!" Jap growled. Hardin nodded and walked away.

The two FNG stood expectantly but Jap went on brushing the crud from his rifle, paying no attention to their presence. The replacements seemed bogged down with a ton of equipment. One was a small man who looked dwarfed by the military equipment he carried. The other was a near-giant of a man who had a permanent scowl. Finally, Boyd asked them the inevitable.

"How many days?"

"How many days what?" the taller of the two men replied.

"Christ, are they making them that dumb?" he asked Jap, who just shrugged indifferently.

"I asked you, how many...?"

Boyd's sentence stopped midstream.

"Take that off!" he ordered sharply.

"Take what off?" the tall man asked.

Boyd put down his M-16, drew his knife from its sheath and stepped up to the soldier, who was a full five inches taller than him. With a quick stoke he cut a cord from around the man's neck. A metallic object fell into his hand.

"What the fuck is this?" he asked.

"None of your business. It's mine," the man answered testily.

Boyd turned and flung the object into Jap's lap. Jap picked it up and pretended to admire it.

"Lovely. A lovely peace symbol," he said, shaking his head. He flung it into a pool of muddy water.

"Boyd waved his knife under the man's nose and roared out a series of questions.

"What are you? Some kind of hippie, yuppie, druggie, commie peacenik? You got a tattoo of Hanoi Jane on your ass? You got a Joan Baez album transplanted in your brain? Well Cherry, this ain't San Francisco. No flower children here. Welcome to the real fucking world. If I ever see you with another piece of shit like that, Charlie won't have to kill you. I'll cut you a second asshole."

"Yeah, well who are you?" the man asked. "The big bad ass around here or something?"

"No, dickhead. I'm just a survivor. You got a hundred zillion days left 'in country'. A survivor is something you'll never be," Boyd replied.

The shorter soldier tried to defuse the atmosphere somewhat by his own introduction.

"I'm Graves," he said. "George Graves."

"Well, that's a cheerie name-Graves!" Boyd replied. "That's something we need around here."

"Sergeant Hardin said you would...uh... get us squared away," the soldier stammered.

"How about I shoot you now, Graves, and save you a lot of trouble?" Boyd retorted.

"What's your problem, anyway?" the tall soldier asked.

"No problem, Cherry," Boyd mocked. "What's your name, anyway?"

"Rickowski."

"Rickowski? Rick-ow-ski? Explains everything. Big dumb fucking Pollacks think they're real hard asses. Well, these little tiny, brown dinks aren't impressed with that. You're just a bigger target to them. Peace symbols don't impress them too much, either."

Jap laid his rifle on a sandbag wall and brought the conversation back into focus.

"Okay, people. Let's talk about some basic shit."

For two days, Boyd tried vigorously to avoid George Graves, whom he aptly nicknamed Gravedigger. The man had decided that Boyd was his hero and role model. It was adoration at first sight. Boyd insulted, ignored and ridiculed the man but to no avail. Gravedigger attached himself to Boyd like a clamp, pestering him with an endless barrage of questions about everything. What was this for? Had Boyd killed many V.C.? How were ambushes conducted? Boyd gave serious thought to blowing up the man with a grenade just to end the suffering.

"Gravedigger, you are the most annoying, dumb shit in the world. I am really looking forward to zipping your worthless butt into a body bag," he said one day, after an hour of questioning. He had tried to escape by cleaning the 50-caliber machine gun on the track but his tormentor had found him.

"Sarge, the mine that killed Youngblood. You didn't explain how it was rigged to go off," the man continued, peering at Boyd over very thick glasses with cheap plastic army frames.

"I'm not a sergeant!" Boyd shouted. "Will you stop calling me 'sarge'? The man's name was Youngblade, not Youngblood. He's dead, that's all you need to know."

"But sarge, how did it work?"

"It went BOOOM," Boyd replied, abandoning the task and climbing down from the machine. He headed for the latrine, hoping the smell would act as a defense. Gravedigger tagged along.

"I enlisted, you know," Gravedigger said. "I wasn't drafted."

Boyd groaned and covered his ears.

In contrast, Rickowski kept to himself, a permanent frown on his face. He did what he was told and nothing more. He didn't ask anyone questions about anything. The other squad members called him Peacenik, but he didn't respond to that. Sometimes they just said, "Hey you." Jap concluded that the soldier was still pissed off because the army recruiter had promised him Fun, Travel and Adventure but hadn't given him all the details.

When a North Vietnamese unit ambushed a convoy taking supplies to a Special Forces camp, the 2-47th was ordered to find and destroy them. The great minds that plan battles, paying no attention to terrain, drew arrows on a map and sent columns of armored vehicles into dense jungle. They packed up and abandoned firebase Emily as quickly as they had created it. The lead tanks broke down the trees and the APCs tried to follow in their path.

Most of the infantry had dismounted and moved through the jungle beside the "highway" which the vehicles were making. It was slow progress, made worse by the fact that they were uprooting trees that were home to hordes of fire ants, wasps and other unfriendly insects. The men were bitten and stung repeatedly until their faces were puffy and red. Their eyes were mere black slits above swollen cheeks.

Boyd walked twenty feet from his track. He kept a constant eye on the trees above him. A sniper could stay concealed up there forever and not be seen. The rain had resumed a determined downpour and visibility was only a few feet. The jungle which had seemed so verdant was now a soupy gray color. It stunk more than usual of rotting vegetation.

Moore had taken the point, walking a dozen feet ahead of the first tank. There was no element of surprise that they were coming. The motors and tracks of their vehicles and the cracking of trees made enough noise to notify Hanoi that a mechanized unit was trying to go through jungle.

Rickowski was behind Moore, followed by Boyd. One the other side of the trail The Pope and Gravedigger were flank security. Kuhn drove the track while Jap manned the 50-caliber. When he looked over, Boyd could see that Gravedigger was plenty scared. He looked like a terrified little boy in a cemetery, with big saucer eyes under the oversized helmet, constantly looking over his shoulder, waving his rifle around like a magic wand that would keep away ghosts. For a brief moment he saw himself, eons ago.

That the operation made no military sense was not lost upon Hardin and Semple. Further back in the column, they were discussing that very point.

"Captain, dis shit doan cut it," Hardin insisted for the tenth time. "Tanks and tracks aren't meant to bust jungle. We blind as bats. Can't see a dink ten feet away."

"I know," Semple replied wearily. "All we're doing is making a road for Charlie. I hope he appreciates it. But what brigade wants us to do is make a big show, a lot of noise, and slowly push them towards the border. There's a special forces unit waiting for them. I don't want to hear any more about it. Just keep the men on their toes."

"Suppose Charlie doan fall for dat?" Hardin persisted. "Suppose dey decide to take us on right here? Fish soup strung out like dis. Dat's us."

"I value your advice, sergeant, but you made your point and you're getting on my nerves," Semple said crisply through pursed lips so the other men couldn't hear. "Go tell those drivers to stop bunching up so much."

An armored vehicle costs hundreds of thousands of dollars. A Russian RPG2 rocket less than one hundred dollars to make. A soldier can learn to use the simple device in a minute. It can penetrate all but the thickest armor plating.

The attack came from the right flank.

The guerrilla lay hidden in dense foliage and let The Pope pass by. Then he slid the tube into his shoulder, looked through the basic sight on the launcher and pulled the trigger. He wheeled and vanished into the jungle almost before the rocket hit.

He had aimed at the armored personnel carrier and from less than thirty feet he seemingly couldn't miss. But Murphy's Law works as well in the jungle as elsewhere. The rocket hit a tree a few feet from the track, just as Gravedigger passed behind it. It exploded with a brilliant flash and powerful bang, scattering metal and wood in every direction. The rest of the squad hit the ground, looking about frantically for the source of the attack, wondering if more would follow. Jap had heard the rocket leave the tube and had started to turn the machine gun when the projectile exploded, causing him to duck down behind the protection of one of the cupolas. When he stuck his head up again, the guerrilla was long gone. The next sound he heard was one he dreaded.

"Medic!"

He recognized The Pope's voice.

"Jap! Stay there and cover us!" Boyd shouted as he sprinted across the trail behind the track. He quickly spied The Pope kneeling over a body. Jap fired short bursts of 50-caliber into the trees above them and into the jungle. If there were snipers as well, the big gun would be a strong deterrent.

"Who is it?" he panted as he dropped beside The Pope, his rifle covering the nearby jungle.

"Gravedigger," came a weak reply.

Boyd glanced quickly at the wounded man, then turned his head away. He was instantly sick.

"C'mon Boyd, fucking help me with this," The Pope insisted.

Boyd laid his M-16 down and fumbled for his first aid kit. He looked again at the wounded man stretched out on the ground.

"Oh shit! Oh, Jesus H. Christ," he said involuntarily, his hands shaking as he fumbled and tried to open a compress package.

It was impossible to tell if the greatest injury had come from the rocket or the flying pieces of tree. There was no mistaking the incredible damage. Gravedigger's right arm was gone from the shoulder down. Most of his chest had been blown open, exposing pieces of smashed and broken ribs. That was not the worst of it.

The right side of the soldier's face was a pulpy mess. His jaw was completely gone, leaving only a cavern-like, gaping hole. He had no tongue and they could see the top of his windpipe. The rest, along with the front of his neck, had been blown away. That the man was blind was obvious. His eye sockets were black holes, a piece of wood protruding from one of them.

He was still alive and making terrible gurgling sounds. His left arm flopped about and he seemed to be trying to raise his head.

Boyd held the puny compress in both hands, with no idea where to put it that would have any use whatsoever. He finally placed it over the man's eye sockets, more to hide the hideousness than to treat any wound. The dark maroon fluid soon seeped through the lily white bandage.

He scarcely heard or felt Wop drop down beside him.

"Oh, shit," was all the medic said as he checked the man's vital signs.

The gurgling noise became louder, like a tiny trapped person inside the soldier's body asking to be released. Each time the man inhaled, his chest made a rasping sound like fingernails on a blackboard. When he exhaled it was a haunting wind accompanied by torrents of blood that shot from his smashed neck. Boyd didn't know a human had so much blood.

"Do something, Wop," The Pope pleaded. "Give him something-anything. Just stop that fucking noise."

The medic stabbed a morphine syringe into the man's chest and pushed the plunger so hard it almost broke. He quickly injected another. They waited a minute, then two, as the sound slowly diminished.

"Aren't you gonna bandage him or something?" The Pope asked.

Wop gave no answer as he gave a third morphine injection just above the heart. The soldier soon became still, his breathing almost stopped.

"No," he finally said. "No need." Then, he sat back on his haunches and looked at the man with a very puzzled expression. "Why do they make bandages white? The blood wouldn't look so bad if the bandages were a dark red or something. Who is he, anyway? I don't know him."

"New guy," Boyd replied. "Graves."

Wop began repackaging his medical kit.

"He gonna make it?" Boyd asked.

"Sometimes your stupidity amazes me," Wop answered. "Bag him. I'll tag him."

Neither of the two confused soldiers moved.

"Bag him, dickhead!" the medic shouted at Boyd as he took the man's dog tag from his boot. "Is that too difficult for you?"

In something of a daze, Boyd went to the track and told Jap to throw down a body bag. Everything was slowly coming into focus.

He nearly collided with Hardin who had run forward when he heard the explosion.

"What yo' got?" the sergeant asked, somewhat out of breath.

"RPG," Boyd replied. "We got one KIA."

"Who?" Hardin asked when he saw the bag.

"Graves," Boyd replied.

"Who's Graves?" Hardin asked.

"The new guy! Jesus, doesn't anybody know the man? He's dead for Christ's sake. He just got wasted and...and...nobody even knows his fucking name!"

"The little fat one or the big one?" Hardin asked, ignoring the outburst.

"Fat one."

"Didn't last long. Hurry up and bag him. We can't sit here all day," Hardin muttered. "Yo' get the dink dat done it?"

"No. Never even saw him," Boyd answered weakly. He had a terrible pain in his head and felt exhausted.

"Don't surprise me none. Dere will be more of 'em, too. We just goddam targets out here," Hardin concluded, and went back to tell the company commander that a man had been killed.

They put Grave's body inside the track and the column started moving again. The word had spread quickly up and down the line and the troops were extremely jittery. Even the tankers were apprehensive about RPG rockets fired at close range. They pulled in the flank security and began spraying the trees with machine gun fire as they lumbered along.

Boyd and The Pope walked just behind the track, trying not to get hit by the "green" trees that were bent back, then suddenly flew up after the track had passed over them. The Pope reached into his shirt pocket, took out something small and square and flung it into the brush.

"Why'd you do that?" Boyd asked.

"I've learned something in Vietnam."

"Like what?" Boyd asked, scanning the trees for snipers.

"How stupid I've been. There's no God. Never was."

"How'd you come to that conclusion?"

"If there was a God, he'd never let this happen. He'd never allow this human carnage. He wouldn't let Youngblade get blown to bits or Knowles die in a crash. He wouldn't let a stupid fat kid like Graves get most of his head blown away."

"That doesn't mean..." Boyd tried to argue.

"Yes it does!" The Pope insisted. "Look, back home, all over America, there are five hundred people in a little church praying for Johnny Jones' safe return. I mean, they are really praying. They are praying so hard their fingers hurt and the blood vessels in their faces break. Then little Johnny gets his fucking head blown off by a communist atheist dink. And they send his body home and these same people all stand around and pray at his grave, saying shit like, 'Well, he's with the Lord now,' or 'It's God's will.' What was the point of all that prayer? Huh? God didn't appear and say, 'Look out, Youngblade. Those bastards put a mine there.' Considering the fact that communists are atheists, God is supposed to be on our side. Either God doesn't listen to prayers or there is no God. But when their prayers are not answered, people make up dumb explanations like 'God works in wondrous ways and He must have a reason.'"

"I hope there's no God," Boyd added.

"Why?"

"Because if there is, when I die I don't know what I'm gonna say to Him."

They broke jungle for three more hours, progressing no more than three kilometers in all. By 1600 hours, the question of where they would establish a base became rather important. Semple tried to impress upon the battalion commander the difficulties they faced. A solution was found in a Daisy Cutter.

A position four clicks from the Cambodian border and one click from their present position was chosen. The column ground to a halt and waited, the men anxiously watching the jungle. At 1700 they heard just a wisp of the sound of the airplane bringing the payload. From just 3000 feet, the crew of the cargo plane pushed the payload out the rear door.

The Daisy Cutter floated slowly towards earth. Its 15,000 pounds of high explosive seemed quite innocuous buried deep within the green canister that swung beneath the parachute. The barometric switches inside constantly gauged the distance to the ground until the container was 150 feet above the earth.

The explosion was impressive by any standard. One soldier described it as a tiny nuclear bomb. The debris came pelting down on them for ten minutes as if it had been expelled by a volcano. There was no question about the direction they were to go.

It took another two hours but finally the lead tank broke into the clearing which the bomb had created. It was littered with broken trees and stumps but it let in the sky and allowed for helicopters to resupply them.

With C4 explosive, chain saws and the dozer blades on two of the tanks, they made the clearing "presentable" within an hour. Chinooks brought them fuel, rations and a water trailer. The Daisy Cutter had also destroyed a large tree that was home to fire ants. Then the helicopter blades picked them up and blew them all over the entire company. They were fighting mad, to say the least, and a full hour was wasted stripping off uniforms, swatting and spraying the tenacious insects who drew blood with every bite.

The rain returned with a sudden ferocity and the world turned dark and dismal. Some men stood in the downpour with a small bar of soap and made some use of the deluge. The feeling of cleanliness was tempered by the necessity of putting on clinging, wet uniforms. They began digging in.

An hour after they began setting up their defensive position, they were surprised by the arrival of fifty Cambodian mercenaries, packed into two Chinooks, accompanied by one American adviser. The Cambodians, like the Vietnamese, were very small men, armed with every ancient hand-me-down weapon manufactured since World War II. Some wore tiger camouflage uniforms, others a mixture of black pajamas and blue jeans. The American adviser was a hard-bitten, tight-lipped man who deflected any serious questions about what his unit did. The men suspected he was CIA, not regular army. He did say to Captain Semple something to the effect that although American units were not allowed to cross into Cambodia, there was nothing wrong with a few homesick Cambodians going home to visit their relatives now and then. He gladly accepted two warm beers and drank them with considerable gusto. He seemed pleased just to hear a few words of English. When asked whether the Cambodians were good soldiers, he replied frankly that they were nothing more than pirates who kill for money.

"We pay them for every V.C. they kill. They cut an ear from each corpse and carry them in a bag. We pay their chief and he, in turn, decides who among his men gets paid what. Any man who wants to become chief can simply challenge the existing chief to a knife fight to the death. This guy is one tough bastard. None of his men is willing to challenge him right now. Don't turn your back on them, though. They're bloody thieves and cut-throats who will kill you in a minute if you have something they want. They work for us because we pay them. If we stopped paying them, or the other side paid them more, they'd kill us without hesitation."

A tiny respite in the gloom arose when the Cambodians saw Hardin shaving in the rain. They collected around him in a circle, all talking loudly at once and gesturing. The American adviser intervened and asked their chief what was the excitement. After much discussion, the adviser laughed heartily and had trouble translating the whole affair into English.

"No offense," he said to Hardin, his palms raised in a peaceful sign, "but they saw the shaving cream on your face and you scraping yourself with the razor. They don't have facial hair and never shave. They don't really understand why some Americans are black and think that with the shaving cream you're turning yourself back into a white man again. They believe you must have magic and want to watch you do it."

Even Hardin found this explanation humorous and broke into peals of laughter. It was contagious. The Americans laughed, then the puzzled Cambodians laughed back, not knowing why but certain that something was funny.

"Sheeeiiit!" was all Hardin could think to say.

Shortly before dark, the Cambodians melted into the jungle, headed towards the border. The Americans never saw or heard anything about them again. Boyd wondered if the day ever came when they didn't get paid and the adviser's ears ended up in the bag.

"There are some jobs I wouldn't want over here," he said to Moore. There was no dispute about that.

The first two days in Firebase Gloria were without serious incident. There was incessant patrolling, digging and filling of sandbags. They received A-rations, water and mail. The artillery soon polluted the air with smoke and cordite until even the food tasted of it. Most of the shells went into Cambodia but no one gave that much serious thought. On the second day, Boyd's squad came across a small bunker and tunnel complex. It appeared to have been used recently and hastily abandoned.

They blew the bunkers with C4 and threw CS grenades into the tunnels. They never expected to find anyone and were completely unprepared when a lone guerrilla, wearing nothing but a thong around his middle, suddenly broke from a hidden tunnel entrance only a few feet from them and made a dash for freedom.

Jap fired his M-16 just as the man dodged left. Moore squeezed off a quick burst just as the man dodged right. Boyd hastily fired high, the bullets going a foot over the man's head. The Viet Cong disappeared into the greenery without so much as a scratch.

At first they were disgruntled, but soon began to shake their heads and chuckle over their atrocious marksmanship.

"Man, what a half-back he'd make," Jap said.

."Sheeiit," Kuhn countered, "you guys were so taken with his naked butt, you didn't have the heart to shoot him."

"I didn't notice you even shooting at him," Boyd replied. "Must have been love at first sight."

By the fourth day, rain and boredom were the main problems. They broke the jungle, searched for the enemy, ate cold rations and tried to fight off the insects. They found trails, the odd strand of broken telephone wire, spent cartridges, unexploded cluster bomb units and bunkers. They found a dismantled bicycle and the base plate for a mortar. But the enemy force had melted away.

They increased the size of their probes to platoon size. The battalion commander was determined to provoke a fight and his plan was to simply offer a big enough piece of bait to make the communists hungry for it.

The process remained the same. Strung out in a line, they hacked at the vegetation, stopped, listened and found nothing. Lieutenant Baxter anointed Rickowski as his radio operator, concluding that the man's size warranted carrying the heavy instrument. Despite repeated warnings from Jap and others, Baxter commanded the searches with a bull-in-a-china-shop method. The man simply couldn't shut up. He talked incessantly, in a loud voice, on the radio-blurting out a torrent of unnecessary chatter.

"What's your sitrep? What's your location? What have you got?" he would ask his squad leaders every few minutes. They generally tried not to answer but that just goaded the officer to call them more often, putting on his most authoritative command voice, making their radios blurt out his messages, giving away their positions. The squad leaders learned it was better to give short, quiet replies.

Rickowski would stand sullenly at Baxter's elbow, handing him the handset whenever it was called for. Baxter seemed to be in a delusion that he was directing a major military offensive.

"That man's a fucking magpie," Moore grumbled as he hunkered down in the bush next to Boyd. They stayed as far away from the "noise box" as possible and worried about an ambush.

"Charlie can hear us coming ten clicks away," Boyd agreed as he squashed a mosquito that was chewing away the back of his wrist. "And that is one dumb pollack standing there with him."

It came to an end the next morning, as they knew it would. The point man came upon a small clearing near a stream and carefully avoided it. The others did the same. Baxter happily saw it as an unexpected benefit. He stood in the clearing and unfolded his map, still protected by its plastic case. He took the handset from Rickowski.

The sharp crack of the sniper's rifle broke through the jungle like a bullwhip. Baxter's helmet flew off and most of his brains spattered all over Rickowski's outstretched arm and shoulder. The officer went backwards like a falling tree, the map case still in his hand. Rickowski didn't move but just looked at his shirt, then at the lieutenant.

The sniper was a professional who had chosen his tree precision with great care. He had an excellent view of the entire clearing but was well-hidden. If his Russian-made sniper rifle had been equipped with a silencer and flash suppresser as well as the high-quality East German telescopic scope, he would have been an even bigger threat. And if he had been content with one kill and had sat still, the Americans never would have seen him. But the sight of Rickowski standing in the open like an enormous block of wood was too tempting for the sniper to pass by. He operated the bolt action of his rifle to take another shot.

Jap's experienced ears had already told him approximately where the sniper was. His eyes didn't miss the tiny bit of movement and sound when the enemy operated the bolt. He rose up and emptied his magazine into the crotch of the tree where the man was concealed, then dashed into the clearing and pushed Rickowski into the protective jungle, the two of them falling on the ground in a gnarl of arms and legs. The man cried out when he landed on the radio strapped to his back. Jap had moved so fast he didn't see or hear the second sniper's bullet snap through the air where the soldier had been standing.

"Anyone see him?" Jap called out to the other squad members.

It was no surprise that there were two snipers around the clearing. The Viet Cong often operated in two-man teams, taking turns shooting from different directions, causing confusion among their potential victims. Jap was sure he had killed the first sniper but it was quite common that neither he nor his weapon had fallen from the tree. A sniper almost always lashed himself to the tree trunk and strung a cord from the wrist to the stock of the rifle.

"I think he's directly south," Kuhn answered in half-whisper.

They waited, listened and watched for another ten minutes, not moving a muscle nor speaking.

"What say, Jap?" Moore finally whispered.

"We cut a choagie," came the answer.

"What about the L.T.?"

"We leave him," Jap replied.

They crawled away, one man at a time, Moore taking the lead. Jap could not get Rickowski to move at all. The man seemed mentally disconnected. Finally, the squad leader stabbed the soldier in the buttocks with his knife then spoke directly into his ear.

"Listen, you worthless shit. You either get moving or I'm going to kill you. I'm not leaving you here alive to tell them how many we are."

The man had seemed paralyzed with fear but the sharp pain in his butt brought some recognition back to his eyes. He got on all fours and crawled like a dog after Boyd. Jap grabbed him by the ankle and shoved his abandoned rifle into his hands.

They worked their way parallel to where

the sniper was hidden, traveling half a kilometer before turning east again. Jap insisted on radio silence until they were almost at the firebase. Jap radioed that they were coming in and that they had one KIA. When Captain Semple learned that they didn't have the body, he was livid. He ordered Jap to turn around and go back and get it. The men looked at each other in astonishment at the order.

"Negative," Jap replied curtly.

"Say again?" came an incredulous response.

"Negative," Jap repeated. "I'm not losing my men trying to recover a body that is lying out in the open. Over."

There was a long, dead silence and they wondered if they had lost radio contact. An order ended that possibility.

"Hellcat six-niner, I'm giving you a direct order. Go back and get that man's body. Over," Semple's voice came through strongly.

Jap looked at the others' faces momentarily and registered their votes of disgust.

"Negative," he said, then turned off the radio.

"I thought that man had some common sense," Moore sputtered.

The word spread quickly that Captain

Semple had charged Jap with insubordination and was calling for a court martial. They were even more galled to learn that he had also added to the charges that Jap had attacked and wounded one of his own men. Rickowski had whined and complained bitterly about the stab wound in his butt, even though Wop said it was superficial. Hardin tried his best to get the whole thing stopped as ludicrous but the company commander was adamant. He was in a near rage about the platoon leader's body left to rot in the jungle.

Hardin risked court martial himself by hounding the captain to drop the whole thing.

"Dat sergeant did the right thing," Hardin insisted. "It would have been irresponsible for him to risk the other men trying to pull a dead body out from under a sniper's nose."

"He had a moral and legal duty to try. It is intolerable to think of the enemy mutilating Lieutenant Baxter's body. His family is at least entitled to have his remains sent home. We do not abandon our dead on the battlefield," the captain insisted.

"We ain't in no classroom situation here," Hardin persisted. "It wouldn't help

Baxter to have other men killed needlessly. Yo' are destroying the morale of dis company."

"And he attacked a member if his squad," Semple added, waving his index finger for emphasis.

"He saved dat man's life. He refused to move when ordered," Hardin corrected the commander.

"He threatened to kill him," Semple countered.

"Which would have been the proper thing to do," Hardin insisted. "Dey couldn't carry him and dey couldn't afford to leave him behind to tell the enemy their size and strength."

"That will be for the court martial panel to decide," was the officer's final word. With a wave of his hand he dismissed Hardin and went back to preparing the report for court martial.

Jap seemed unperturbed by the uproar. He even saw the positive side of it.

"Hell, a court martial can take days. I have to have time to meet with my defense lawyer. I could use a few days back at Bearcat. You guys are my witnesses. You have to come back, too. We can have a party. With luck, we can stretch this into a couple of weeks. I wish I had thought of this before."

"They may send your ass to prison at Fort Leavenworth. Or they have a stockade up at Long Binh. You might have to do time right here," Moore suggested in a more sobering tone.

"I was wrong about Semple. I thought he was okay. Instead, he's a fucking idiot," Boyd added. A quiet anger kept growing inside him over the injustice of it all. "If he wants that fat shit's body, let him go get it."

"I don't think you can tell the court martial panel a captain is an idiot," Moore suggested. "Even if it is true."

"Baxter was an idiot. He was a walking target," Kuhn added. "They don't come any dumber, except maybe that pollack. You shoulda just left him standing there, Jap. We might have got that second sniper, too."

"Too late now," Jap agreed. "Semple had Peacenik transferred right out of here. Hardin says he got him a desk job at division headquarters. Air-conditioned office, the whole bag."

"You shitting me?" Boyd asked.

"No. He's already gone," Jap assured him.

"Son-of-a-bitch."

"He got his combat infantry badge," Jap added.

"Son-of-a-bitch."

The decision to abandon Firebase Gloria was no surprise. If the Viet Cong and North Vietnamese had been in the area recently, they had long since slipped back into Cambodia. All the battalion had to show for its efforts was one dead sniper, and even that wasn't confirmed. Eight Americans had died and eleven more had been seriously wounded. On the big electronic scoreboard in Saigon, the "body count" clerks sputtered and fumed about the poor showing. At the nightly news briefing, an aging colonel tried to put a good face on the operation saying that major enemy supply routes and supply dumps had been destroyed. Waving his pointer, the colonel insisted that the enemy had suffered a major setback. The reporters yawned, filed their reports, then went off to the hotel bar to get quietly drunk.

The Chinooks came and lifted out the artillery battery while the infantry maintained their guard. Bunkers were filled in and sandbags emptied.

It was late afternoon when they finally got the order to roll. The engineers had worked ahead, scanning the trail they would use for mines. With the tanks in the lead, they rumbled towards Highway 1, looking forward to some rest, hot food and showers, and cold beer. At 1900 hours they hit the asphalt of the highway and turned south towards Saigon. A military police jeep fell into the convoy just behind the second tank, a sergeant talking to his counterpart in the Vietnamese National Police.

The withdrawal was well-organized. The traffic at each intersection was blocked by police jeeps as the tanks and tracks rolled through without stopping. Boyd almost felt a sense of superiority as they passed by these roadblocks. It was as if they were celebrities or foreign dignitaries being escorted to an important meeting. He impulsively tossed some C-rations to a group of kids standing along the road and watched them scramble for them.

It was 2200 hours when they reached the outskirts of Saigon. They noticed the increased number of buildings and vehicles but paid little attention to them. The convoy took a different route than the one they had used going north. The major road was being used by another convoy, also headed south. The police were busy trying to prevent any traffic jams.

In another two hours they would have reached Bearcat without incident if it had not been for a traffic accident. Their route took them through a densely-populated section of the city where the traffic control was now the responsibility of the "white mice." There were so many pedicabs, motorbikes and bicycles that the police had their hands full clearing the way for Sheridan tanks clipping along at 30 m.p.h. The accident still might not have happened at all if two police officers had not completely abandoned their post to go into a bar and pick up a bribe. They were sure they had plenty of time before the convoy actually arrived. They were off by nearly ten minutes.

The driver of the lead tank scarcely saw the brightly-painted pedicab that came out of a side street directly in his path. Although tanks can stop in surprisingly short distances, there was no chance in this case.

The left track hit the puny cab directly in the side, flinging the two passengers out of the seat and sending them rolling along the pavement like logs. The driver went the other way, landing on top of the tank momentarily before flipping off to the pavement. The cab spun down the street like a crumpled beer can until it hit a man on a motorbike, nearly killing him.

The crash alerted the errant policemen who rushed from the bar, blowing whistles and shouting orders at the pedestrians. It didn't take them long to grasp what had happened. Angrily they began shouting at the tank driver and one drew his pistol and waved it menacingly at the soldier's head. The tank commander pulled an M-16 from inside the tank and pointed it at the policeman. A small crowd of Americans and Vietnamese came out of the bar to see what was the excitement.

The convoy of armored vehicles had come to a dead halt, their powerful motors idling, the troops wondering what had caused them to stop. If there was an opportune time and place for an accident to occur, this was not it.

Sitting motionless as they were, the troops could better survey the city and its occupants. They did not like what they saw.

Young Vietnamese men, obviously of draft age, dressed in immaculate white shirts and dark pants, were walking about or riding on new Japanese motorbikes. Most had a woman on their arm or perched on the back of their bikes, long silk dresses blowing back as the riders made their way in and out of traffic.

The convoy had stopped in the middle of Saigon's nightclub district. Neon lights abounded, advertising bar girls and booze. There were no doors on the bars, just strings of beads that formed a partial barrier. The sound of loud rock music seemed to come from every nook and cranny, overpowering even the noise of the motorbikes. American soldiers, in Hawaiian shirts and Bermuda shorts, wandered along the streets, stopping to look curiously at the convoy before ducking into the next bar.

"Tough war, huh?" Kuhn said in disgust.

"How come these dinks aren't in the army?" Moore asked aloud. "Christ, we draft our kids at eighteen and these bastards are older than that. Just one big goddam party for them while we fight their war for them."

There might not have been any further problems at all if Boyd had not spied the American on the balcony. Something caught his eye and his nostrils at the same time. On the second floor, he focused on a man standing next to a bar-b-que, a large fork in one hand and a can of beer in the other. A Vietnamese woman wearing some sort of flimsy nightgown was standing next to him, gazing at the combat troops with mild interest. The man seemed to sense Boyd looking at him and gave a small wave with his beer can in some sort of salute. It wasn't an insult at all, just a greeting. But it was the proverbial spark that lit the fuse.

Boyd calmly reached down and took a can of ham and lima beans from a C-rations box. He removed his helmet, stood up and pulled up his shirt sleeve. The other squad members watched him with curious expressions, then turned to identify his intended target.

"Bar-b-que this, you bastard!" Boyd shouted as he let fly. His aim was not perfect but it was fairly good. He missed the soldier but hit the woman directly in the forehead. She clasped her hands to her head as blood spurted from a deep gash. The soldier didn't retreat but pointed at Boyd and shouted something that was probably a challenge of some sort. This was greeted by Boyd's next missile, a smoke grenade. It flew straight past the man's head and into the apartment behind. Soon purple smoke began billowing from the opening. It was completely harmless but was effective enough to persuade the man and his whore to retreat.

The other squad members caught the spirit of the occasion. Kuhn accurately placed a CS-grenade through the door of the apartment. That could not be called harmless and would drive most of the occupants from the building in minutes. Kuhn celebrated with a powerful Rebel Yell that carried half the length of the convoy.

The depth of rage and resentment was deeper than anyone realized. From vehicle to vehicle the word spread until the entire company caught on to the game. They all stood up on the tops of the tracks and began throwing everything they could lay their hands on. Vietnamese on motorbikes ran a hail of C-ration cans that more than just raised bruises. Some riders were knocked to the pavement by the impact. The bars were the recipients of smoke grenades and CS-grenades that flew easily through the strings of beads and burst inside. The powerful tear gas soon had patrons streaming into the streets for air, only to be hit with C-ration cans. Some women screamed and male voices hurled curses. A few Americans paused long enough to at least consider throwing something back or even climbing on the tracks to have a fist fight, but they quickly forgot the idea when the first shots were fired.

Jap, having tired of the throwing game, put his M-16 on single shot and began systematically shoot out the light bulbs on a large neon sign. He shot away the large bulbs around the edge, then shot the tits off the outline of a woman pouring champagne into a glass.

The idea was an instant hit and the streets emptied in a hurry as more and more soldiers took up the new target practice. The Vietnamese police vanished just as quickly as the civilians. As each neon sign went totally dark, the Rebel Yell was heard again and again.

In his command track, Captain Semple was shouting in his radio for everyone to stop firing, but he got no answer. Finally, he dispatched Hardin towards the front of the convoy and he ran towards the rear, shouting orders as loudly as he could. No one paid him the slightest attention. When a soldier in fourth platoon opened fire on a billboard on top of a building with an M-60 machine gun, the officer nearly fainted. Hardin caught up with him. The sergeant had only been able to get one squad to stop shooting and as soon as he had left, they started again.

"We have a mutiny here, sergeant!" Semple shouted.

"Yo' bet yo' ass we do and we damned well better get out of here before someone is killed," Hardin answered. Without waiting for further instructions, he raced to the lead tank and ordered the driver to drive on. The man said something about not leaving the scene of the accident but Hardin was having none of it. He pointed his M-16 at the man's head.

"I said, drive!"

The soldier was duly impressed and gave the engine full throttle so quickly Hardin scarcely had time to jump free. Before he reached the next intersection, the tank had eclipsed all its previous speed records.

Each driver, in turn, began to roll, forcing the infantry to sit down or fall off. They did so with a sense of elation and accomplishment they had not felt in weeks.

"Saigon's a fun town!" Kuhn shouted to the others. "Do you think they'll invite us back?"

Sitting on top of his command track, Captain Semple just hung his head in his hands and moaned.

"Shit! Shit! Shit!" he said over and over again. "They're gonna court martial my ass for sure. There goes my military career. There goes my political career. What am I gonna tell my father?"

Five intersections away, a military police jeep was parked in the middle of the street. The two Americans MP's had heard the shooting but had no idea who had been doing it. They carried out their standard operating procedures to block off the street.

As they saw the lead tank approaching, its driving lights on, they signaled with red flashlights for it to stop. When it was fifty feet away, they realized that was not going to happen and ran for their lives.

The tank hit the jeep broadside and flipped it into the air. It bounced twice before the tank hit it again, this time rolling right over it. The second tank also hit and flattened it a bit further. The third track sent it spinning into a telephone pole.

When the military police dared to venture out from a side street, they got a scant glimpse of the last track and its markings. One of the soldiers sitting on top waved to them.

"Goddam Ninth Infantry-again," was all one of them could think to say.

His companion was troubled by something else: "Who's gonna pay for that jeep?"

Day 253. Camp Bearcat. The whole company is confined to barracks while the division commander tries to decide what to do about us. Captain Semple was relieved and is gone. We don't know where and don't really care. These investigators keep asking us who did what and no can remember. I said I heard shooting from the rear of the convoy but don't know who did it. They didn't believe me, but so what? Kuhn said he thought there were snipers on the rooftops and maybe some of the guys in fourth platoon shot at them. The Pope told them the devil had something to do with it but he wasn't sure what. There's some scuttlebutt going around that the Ninth Infantry is permanently barred from Saigon and the commanding general got a strip taken off his ass personally by Westmoreland. The good news is that talk about a court martial for Jap has been completely forgotten. The bad new is that they also shit all over Hardin. Semple's last act was to blame him. The division commander gave him an Article 15 and took a stripe from him for "failure of leadership and discipline" or some such bullshit. Hardin took it well. Didn't say a word, just saluted the general, did an about face and left. But we know it really hurt him. You can see it in his eyes. He's a lifer. It took him six years to win that last stripe. Goddam army. It wasn't his fault. There was nothing he could do but the Army has to blame someone at the bottom. They said he might even have to pay for the jeep that was demolished. Shit, they'd have to take half his pay for twenty years. He's always given the army 200% and they screwed him. We all told him we're sorry. If we had known they'd blame him, we wouldn't have done it. He didn't say anything, just walked away. Even though we're confined to our hootches, we've been sneaking plenty of booze in every night. The brothers in the 2-39th are bringing it over right under the MP's noses. They're only charging us cost, too. Rather decent of them, knowing how they could screw us. We're not even allowed to see the bad movies they usually show in the mess hall. Now that's really cruel. The Pentagon got a long letter from Knowles's father. He wrote and asked if they can tell him anything about his son. He's listed as Missing in Action. The Pentagon sent it to the division and the division sent it down here. No one will answer it. Jap asked me if I wanted to but I said no. He let it go at that. I got to thinking about Graves one night. I realized I didn't care

one bit about him getting killed. Same with
Baxter. I was almost glad. He was a jerk
and when a jerk gets wasted, I don't feel
for him. He could get us all killed. I wish
that bastard Rickowski had bought it, too.
There's a rumor that Olive Oyl is running a
bar and bowling alley in Saigon. He stole
the bowling alley right off the docks. It was
packed in four huge crates and he just as-
sembled it. It was supposed to go to some
air base. A trooper from the Cav. says he
ran into him and he said to tell us to come
up to Saigon and we'll have a real blow-
out. Now that would be something to see.
They put Wop in the hospital for a while.
He was acting really weird. A guy was in
the Aid Center for some minor thing and
Wop tried to remove his kidney or some
such shit. Jap went to see him and said
he's okay at times, then starts talking
crazy. The doctors think he's faking it just
'cause he wants to get sent home. Jap told
them Wop wouldn't do that. The man hasn't
been right for a long time. Apparently he
also wrote a letter home that was totally
crazy. It said things about killing men and
eating human parts and stuff like that. His
parents freaked out and went straight to
their congressman with it. Things really
started happening after that. I think I'll try

that. Maybe I'll get Wop to write it for me. We got cookies from kids in a grade school in Indiana. We had to write letters back saying how much we appreciated them. Nice gesture and everything but the damned things were so dry we couldn't eat them. I also got a letter from some high school girl I've never heard of. My mother gave her my address and said I'd really like to have some mail. She asked a bunch of dumb questions. I get the feeling she's doing this for some kind of school essay. I threw it away. I'm having trouble even remembering what my home town is like. Or why anyone would want to live there. Or what I'm gonna do when I get out of here. If I get out of here. I have trouble focusing on anything.

Chapter 5
SHADOWS

DAY 249. Camp Bearcat. Our little incident in Saigon seems to have generally been swept under the carpet. The news media didn't seem to pick up on it so the division commander let it drop. The brigade commander had the entire battalion formed up and gave us a lecture about discipline and the important traditions of the U.S. Army. Actually it was a pretty good speech, even though we had to stand in the sun to hear it. Maybe there was a time when we actually would have believed that shit. Then he gave out some medals which, I guess, showed there were no hard feelings on his side. He also dropped the restrictions and we were able to get to the PX and the Class VI for some booze. There's a rumor that Hank Snow will entertain here soon. Doubtful any of the combat units will get to see

the show. Most of the entertainment is for
the REMF. This is such a tough war for
them, they need the relaxation. They kicked
Wop out of the hospital, saying he was just
faking combat fatigue or something. Man,
they oughta run some real tests on him
sometime. The man has more morphine in
his body than blood. He shakes real bad,
talks to himself and has a permanent case
of the shits. Hardin's mood swings between
really worrying about Wop to kicking his
butt. The battalion surgeon has written him
off. They used to be thick as thieves but
now the doc has washed his hands of Wop.
Says he's so drug-addicted and screwed
up he could never be a doctor. Wop says it
doesn't matter any more because he
doesn't want to be a doctor anyway. Well,
wonder of wonders. Hardin was due for
re-enlistment and said no. He has 18 years
in and is giving it up. That blew the re-enlistment officer's mind! Hardin said he can't
support a war he no longer believes in, and
he doesn't trust the army anymore. Said
he wants to go home and fight for the rights
of blacks in the U.S. That scares the hell
out of me because I don't want Hardin fighting for any cause that might suddenly come
after me. Jap has become a loner. The blow-
out with his family has really messed him

up good. They don't write to him anymore. He tries to pretend it doesn't matter but his family was his heart and soul. I can't understand how a family could disown a son who lays his life on the line in the service of his country and then kiss the butt of some smart shit who refused to do it. Go figure. The brigade commander kept talking about duty, honor, country. I wanted to shout, "Hey man, maybe that's what America used to stand for, but no more. The only rule now is: Every man for himself and only the very, very stupid serve." Everybody is just thinking about staying alive and going home. Except Moore. He never talks about going home. Says he tried it once and it was a downer. Now he talks about going to Canada, Africa or Australia to live. As long as it is really remote-no people. He said he doesn't want to be an American anymore. I never thought about it quite that way but it kinda makes sense. Moore said he just doesn't want to be around people again. Animals, okay. Animals are honest. He wants a cabin, a horse, a dog and a woman. And a gun-to shoot anyone who comes near him. But at least Moore wants to talk about it. The other brothers don't want to talk at all-about anything. Each man just retreats to a corner of the hootch

*and drinks alone. The Pope has started
wearing his helmet and his flak jacket all
the time. He's scared shitless but doesn't
know what he is afraid of. He's walking
around base camp with the damn things
on! Hardin asked him why but he just
walked away. He even laces the flak jacket
up in the front. He must be melting in there.
I have my doubts this company can fight
anymore.*

The end of the investigation and restrictions lifted a dark curtain from the men of the 2-47th. They suddenly received fresh fruit, hamburgers, hot dogs and reconstituted chocolate milk that had a peculiar chemical taste. Some men seemed to eat non-stop while others had no appetite at all. Boyd was one who had little appetite and was content to drink large amounts of Budweiser.

He had a sudden sense of disconnection and wandered about constantly, going from hootch to hootch as if he was looking for something or someone. He couldn't sit still for more than a few minutes. He lost a few bucks in a poker game in which Moore displayed an uncanny ability to cheat. Everyone knew he was cheating because he told them he was, but they could not figure out how he did it. The Pope showed no interest in cards or anything else but had taken to drawing pictures on a large yellow pad. He sat on his cot, sweat running down his face from under his helmet, the top of his pants soaked with sweat dripping from under the flak jacket. He doodled incessantly, with almost frantic motions, drawing everything from landscapes to faces. He drew cartoon characters and geometric patterns. He printed words, then drew fancy boxes around them. None of it made any sense and none of it was very good, but he reacted protectively if anyone tried to look at his art. He did impulsively fasten one drawing to the center tent pole. It was the helmeted face of a soldier, face so emaciated it looked like a skull, eyes very dark and sunken, seeming to stare at a crucifix dangling in front of his eyes. The caption below read:

NINTH INFANTRY DIVISION PRAYER
Yea, though I walk through the Valley
of the Shadow of Death,
I shall fear no evil,
'Cause I'm the meanest son-of-a-bitch
in the Valley.

Moore later moved out of the hootch because he said he didn't like being near a guy who might kill him in his sleep because he heard voices or something calling for human sacrifice. Kuhn soon followed and The Pope had the place all to himself.

In his meandering, Boyd wandered into Hardin's hootch, something he would not have had the courage to do months earlier. Somehow, since he hadn't re-upped, Hardin seemed less intimidating, almost human. He found the man sitting on his cot, reading.

"You can read?" Boyd joked.

"Yo' think a po' nigger from Alabama can't read?" Hardin asked back. He seemed genuinely glad to have the company.

"Just a joke," Boyd replied, dropping down on the end of the cot.

"Wanna drink?" Hardin asked, holding out a whiskey bottle. "Jack in da Black." He slurred his words enough for Boyd to know that most of the bottle had been consumed.

Boyd decline the offer and picked up the book Hardin had been reading. The stamp inside the cover said it had come from the camp recreation centre. It was a collection of poems.

"You read this?" he asked.

"No, I just look at da pictures," Hardin shot back, snatching the book from Boyd's hand.

"I had to read that stuff in high school," Boyd continued, trying to smooth any irritation. "Hated it. I didn't mind reading it, but then we had to tell what it meant. What the author was trying to say. Shit like that. Maybe the author didn't mean anything. Maybe he was fuckin' stoned out of his mind. Maybe he was just trying to make a buck and this was the only was he could do it. Why do we always try to know why someone does something? Who really gives a shit? He did it."

"Po little white chile," Hardin smirked. "I never went to no high school."

"You got a favorite poem?" Boyd asked, crumpling the beer can in his fist and tossing it into a corner. Hardin didn't seem to mind the poor housekeeping practice.

"Yeah. Dis one," the sergeant replied, turning several pages, then handing the book to Boyd. "Read it and tell me what dat man is puttin' down."

Boyd took the book and squinted at the words. The print was very small and his eyesight was somewhat beer sodden. He skipped over the introductory passages about the author's life. He had at least heard of Rudyard Kiplin.

TOMMY

I went into a public-house to get a pint o' beer,
The publican 'e up an' sez, "We serve no redcoats here."
The girls behind the bar they laughed an' giggled fit to die,
I outs into the street again an' to myself sez I:
O it's Tommy this, an' Tommy that, an' Tommy go away,
But it's "Thank you, Mister Atkins," when the band begins to play,
The band begins to play, my boys, the band begins to play
O it's "Thank you Mister Atkins," when the band begins to play.
Yes, making mock o' uniforms that guard you while you sleep
Is cheaper than them uniforms, an' they're starvation cheap;
An' hustling drunken soldiers when they're goin' large a bit
Is five times better business than paradin' in full kit.
Then it's Tommy this, an' Tommy

that, an' "Tommy, ow's your soul?"
But it's "Thin red line of 'eroes" when
the drums begin to roll
The drums begin to roll my boys, the
drums begin to roll,
O it's "Thin red line of 'eroes" when
the drums begin to roll.

There was more to the poem but Boyd stopped reading.

"I dunno," he continued. "What's Rudy trying to say?"

Hardin smiled and tapped his finger against his temple.

"Yo' honkies ain't so smart," he said. "He's a white man. Can't yo' understand yo' own people? 'Tommy' is the British G.I. Joe. He's saying dat in time of war, folks love soldiers and treat dem like heroes. In time of peace, dey treat dem like dog shit and won't even let dem set foot in a bar. They treat 'em all like niggers."

"Yeah?" Boyd challenged the theory. "Well, the author isn't exactly up to date. Now civilians hate us all the time." He changed his mind and drank some of Hardin's whiskey. Then he abruptly changed topics.

"How come you didn't re-up? You got about a zillion years in. Couple more, you'd

get a pension, a gold watch or something.
Why throw it all in now?"

"Yo' my new Career Counselor?" Hardin
asked testily.

"Just wondering."

Hardin was about to reply to that statement when he caught on to the joke. He
swung his feet around and sat up straight.

"I told dem all a buncha sheer bullshit,"
he admitted. "Real reason is for da first
time, I'm scared."

"We all are," Boyd replied, rather confused by the statement.

"No, I mean really scared. I doan mean
afraid, nervous, tense or any of dat shit.
I'm talking 'bout deep down, right to da
soul, boot-shaking, sick to my stomach,
piss yo' pants scared! I can't function no
more. First sound, I freeze up."

"I've never seen you freeze up," Boyd
disputed the sergeant's analysis.

"Yo' watching me every minute? Yo' inside my mind? My body? I'm paralyzed half
the time. My legs turn to lead. Can't move.
Can't speak. Can't think. I gotta get out. I
just hope no gets killed 'cause of me."

"I never knew that," Boyd said quietly.
"When shit starts happening, you're the
one who knows what to do. You always
tell us what to do. When things are get-

ting out of hand, we rely on you."

"No more," Hardin shook his head, looking Boyd straight in the eye. "Not any longer. Doan rely on me. Doan wait for me. Take care of yo'self. Now, get da fuck outa here. Yo' can take da book if yo' want."

Boyd left Hardin's hootch very distressed. A strong man-a giant of a man-seemed broken and free falling. If Hardin couldn't keep his shit together, what chance had the rest of them? Even though Hardin didn't pledge him to secrecy, he decided not to say anything to the others. Everyone had enough problems. He went to the mess hall and bummed a cup of coffee from one of the cooks. He sat down at a table and thumbed the pages of the book of poetry. It kept him interested for less than five minutes and he left it on the table and walked out. If Hardin got an overdue book fine, meticulously calculated by the little, anal-retentive REMF at the base book exchange, it probably wouldn't make a big impact on his life.

The American forces in Vietnam were not without their allies. Two Korean divisions contributed considerably to the war effort and the Australian and New Zealand governments sent small, but effective, fighting units. The Aussies were given an area of operation in the southern part of Vietnam, an inhospitable, jungle-covered range of mountains that ten divisions could not possibly secure. The Australians didn't need or welcome American help. They operated well, mostly in small units, and practiced a unique style of counter-guerrilla warfare similar to that which the British had developed in Malaya. Joint American-Australian operations were more for the publicity of demonstrating unity and cooperation then necessity.

The supply line from the port of Vung Tau north to Long Binh and Saigon was an extremely important one. It could never be made completely safe, and convoy security was a perpetual task. Occasionally, large Viet Cong units completely cut the road or fired rockets into the port itself. Once Viet Cong frogmen sank a ship that had just arrived from the Philippines, sending thousands of cases of beer to the bottom. It was a military disaster.

The U.S. command responded by spraying the jungle with defoliant and cutting the dead trees back from the highway nearly 500 feet, using bulldozers and Rome plows to make it tougher for the communists to ambush the vehicles with any accuracy. The highway was paved and iron grates were welded over all culverts to prevent the placement of mines under the road. None of these efforts, by themselves, could stop the guerrillas. It still required troops making endless search and destroy "sweeps" through the vast, inhospitable country to keep the enemy on the defensive.

The 2-47th was a poor choice of units to operate in the area. The terrain was impossible for tracked vehicles and the rain had turned trails into muddy swamps and streams into rivers. Nor could vehicles go up the mountains, but had to confine their movements to the valleys between. The unit was badly under-strengthed. Some squads only had four or five men. Boyd's platoon had no lieutenant so Jap was still acting platoon leader. None of these simple facts prevented the American battle planners from sending the two companies of the battalion south to link up with an Australian unit to seek out an enemy force that had blown a bridge into a pile of gravel and ambushed an engineer unit that came to rebuild it. The Americans would be under Australian command. Only two hours before they left Bearcat, they received a new company commander, a captain who had been chained to a desk job at brigade headquarters and who had been clamoring for a combat assignment. Captain Morrow had rushed to his new command so quickly that he had no time to even acquire maps of where they were going. He wisely relied on Hardin to organize their move.

It didn't take the Australian brigadier long to realize he'd been sent the wrong type of unit. He had established a firebase with two New Zealander-"Kiwi"-artillery batteries, one American battery. He had requested a "leg" outfit, not a mechanized one. He bluntly told the American commanders their men would be walking.

"Those vehicle are nothing but a nuisance to me," he said in a crisp voice. "Just park them."

There was scant time for socializing. The Aussies quickly sought out the Americans to barter their Fosters ale for Marlboro or Winston cigarettes. They were a rugged bunch, wearing floppy bush hats, speaking a twangy language that roughly resemble English-phrases filled with words such as "mate" and ending with an inflection that gave the impression every sentence was really a question. Boyd guessed that the word "mate" had two meanings. It meant "my absolutely best friend whom I'd give my life for" and it also meant "Hey! I'm talking to you." It was all in the pronunciation. The men of 1st R.A.R. were incredibly self-confident and were undaunted by the Viet Cong whom they referred in the most contemptuous terms. In general, they were much older than the Americans, a characteristic of volunteer army. The ale tasted funny, but it would do.

The Australians streaked their faces with camouflage paint, a practice the Americans had long since abandoned, and traveled very light. One soldier had his own unique camouflage. He had caught a huge, hairy, yellow spider, as big as a tarantula, then tied a string around one of its legs. The other end of the string he had sewed to his hat. The spider could walk all around the top of the man's head but no further, as his "leash" wouldn't let him escape. Another man had done the same with a rhino beetle, an "armor-plated" beetle bigger than a golf ball. The insect seemed to love the beer the soldier held in his cupped hand.

"Drunken little sot, he is," the soldier declared.

The Americans thought they knew something about the inhabitants of jungle but they had never seen creatures such as these. It gave them a creepy feeling.

The Aussies were appalled when they saw the American's flak jackets.

"You wear this bloody thing in the jungle?" one sergeant asked as he tested the weight of it, then threw it down in disgust. "You won't be wearing it long in these parts then, mate."

The brigadier didn't approve of troops lolly-gagging around. He seemed to be everywhere, his "dog robber," as the men called his Aide-de-camp, in tow. Boyd realized the Aussie troops were terrified of this small but imposing man. Whenever he came near them, they stiffened into ramrod steel posts and shouted "Yessir" like they really meant it. He wondered what punishments could be handed out to someone who screwed up, or who said, "Up yours, mate," to an Australian general. The general even made Boyd nervous, although he never spoke directly to American soldiers about anything.

By the first evening nearly all of the Australian troops had gone into the jungle. The brigadier wanted the American forces out early the next morning. The artillery batteries were firing at a high rate, lobbing volley after volley of high explosives at targets called in by small teams of their spotters on some of the mountain tops. The gunners were straining at their guns as if World War II was being re-enacted. Boyd watched them for a while, counting the movements it took to fire a shell, eject the brass, reload and fire again. There was a hum-drum, endless routine to it that was tiring just to watch.

Bravo Company had a very basic mission. It would move to a mountain top five clicks from the firebase, then actively search the area for tunnels or Viet Cong base camps. It didn't take long to realize how difficult the task would be. Within an hour they were in dense jungle that covered hills so steep they had to pull each other up the slopes. The fact that the ground had turned to a paste of mud and rotting vegetation made the task doubly difficult. They had been ordered to wear their flak jackets and the Aussie's warning was prophetic. The heat built up and, combined with the tremendous effort required to climb, the troops were worn down in a matter of hours. Bravo Company had three cases of heat exhaustion before 1400 hours. The illness struck without the slightest warning. Soldiers just felt dizzy, experienced a rush of sweat through every pore, then became limp rags and fell down. Wop stripped their equipment and shirts away and poured water over them to get their temperatures down. It was a tremendous sacrifice for other men to give up their water, as they were all running dangerously low. They made crude stretchers from poncho liners and dragged the sick men up and down the hills, four men to a stretcher, each holding a corner. This dead weight put an extra strain on the already-fatigued soldiers. They also had to carry the extra rifles and equipment.

Captain Morrow soon became the fourth heat exhaustion case. He had valiantly tried to stick it out, eating handfuls of salt tablets and rationing his water as best he could, but his long stretch of duty in an air-conditioned office had left him completely unprepared for such an arduous trek. Hardin was left in command once again and gave his first order immediately: "Sit down and throw away those goddam flak jackets!"

It was a tremendous relief but too late to give them back their sapped vitality. Some men also threw away their helmets which trapped the heat against their heads. They shed half their sandbags, radio batteries, rations and every object that seemed to weigh them down. The Pope refused to give up his flak jacket, even after Jap ordered him to do so. Finally, Jap gave up but said that if The Pope got heat exhaustion, no one was going to carry him. They would leave him.

They couldn't find a single clearing in the jungle for resupply or medevac but a tiny stream afforded them some precious water. It also slowed them down even more because it took each man five minutes or more to fill his canteens from the trickling water.

Moore had the most experience in the jungle and took the point. He would pull himself a few feet up a slope, using tree trunks or roots as a hand-hold, then watch and listen. The other men tried to time their moves so when he stopped they did. Otherwise, they made so much noise behind him he couldn't hear.

It was an hour after he had taken the point that Moore stopped and froze, his body bent over hugging the side of the hill to make as low a profile as possible. The men behind gave quick hand-signals and the entire column froze. Five minutes went by before Jap wiggled up beside him.

"What?" he whispered.

Moore shook his head in disbelief and gave a little shrug.

"A kid," he whispered back. "I saw a little boy, about four years old, just standing up there, looking at me. Then he disappeared."

"No fuckin' way," Jap refuted the idea. "There's no villages here. What would a kid be doing in the middle of this shit?"

"I tell you I saw him," Moore insisted.

"You're seeing shadows, man," Jap insisted. "Shadows or ghosts. A man has to constantly strain his eyes to see in this hellhole."

"I saw a dink!" Moore insisted.

"Maybe it was a monkey," Jap suggested. "You better take a break."

Jap moved Moore further back in the column and Boyd took the point. Twenty minutes later, he gave a sharp hand signal and they stopped again, tense eyes peering into the dark green-gray sea of trees and vines. Every man had the word "ambush" in his brain. All they heard was the buzz of some insect.

Jap moved slowly up the hill until he reached the heel of Boyd's boot. He gave a tug and Boyd slid down beside the platoon leader.

"What you got?" Jap asked.

"A little kid. I about blew him away. Scared the shit out of me. I didn't see or hear nothing, then suddenly he was there. Just looking at me, curious-like. You know?"

"Not you, too," Jap complained. I thought Moore was cracking up. Now everybody is seeing shit."

"I saw him."

"So, where is he now?"

"He just disappeared."

"Disappeared, my ass. You musta heard what Moore said. You saw a shadow," Jap replied. "Nobody lives here. There are no kids here."

"I know what I saw," Boyd persisted.

"Mass fuckin' hysteria. Just what I need. Okay, I'm goin' back and tell Hardin 'bout this. But keep moving."

"Yeah, well tell him this place is haunted," Boyd added.

"I know that will impress him," Jap said.

After Jap had slipped away, Boyd rubbed the little statue in his shirt pocket.

"Bubba, I hope you're good for keeping away spirits," he muttered, then once again began crawling up the hill.

All the while they were struggling

against the mountains, a helicopter whirled overhead and an irate Australian operations officer nattered over the radio that Hardin was not moving fast enough. He was hours away from his objective and must reach it before night fall. Hardin replied that they were doing their best but if the complainer wanted to come down and show them a better way, he would be welcome. Hardin asked the officer to find even a small opening in the jungle for medevac but was told that there was none. They couldn't even "shithook" the men out on slings lowered by cable from Chinook helicopters.

At 1800 hours, they reached the base of the mountain, or at least Hardin thought that's where they were. It was extremely hard to navigate and he had to call for the artillery battery to fire some air bursts (marking rounds) at different grid intersections to get a proper compass bearing. He couldn't see the shells explode, but heard them.

"We can't go any further today," Jap panted as he and Hardin considered their options. "We certainly can't carry these sick men up that mountain tonight."

"Yo' got a point dere, judge," Hardin agreed. "Dat general and friends can stick it up dere collective asses if dey thing we gonna try. Dis is it."

"We dig in?"

"No," Hardin replied, taking a small drink of water from his canteen and resisting the urge to drink it all. "Men's too tired. Too noisy. Just circle the wagons."

The weary troops were pleased with the pronouncement that they would not have to spend the next three or four hours digging foxholes. They were simply assigned sectors of a defensive circle. They set out their Claymore mines and cut down some brush to clear better fields of fire. They ate a meal of cold C-rations and cleaned their weapons. Hardin wouldn't let them smoke. The smell could carry long distances and acted like a beacon to their location. The men grumbled but complied.

The evening rain storm came as sure as Old Faithful and they huddled under poncho liners and crushed the mosquitoes on their hands and faces. They talked in whispers and tried to pass the time. Boyd and Moore were teamed together, a dozen yards from Kuhn and The Pope.

"We both saw that kid," Boyd said. "No one is supposed to live out here. Whaddya make of it?"

Moore stared straight ahead for several minutes, not answering. He was trying to get the last bit of taste out of a chiclet. He seemed troubled by the riddle.

"Not sure," he finally replied, "but I got a theory. And I don't like it."

"What theory?" Boyd asked.

"The kid appears and disappears like a ghost. Disappears to...where? The only explanation that makes sense is a tunnel."

"Here?"

"Anywhere. Everywhere," Moore answered. Have you ever heard of the tunnels of Cu Chi?"

"No, what about them?"

"The 25th has its base camp at Cu Chi. We built the base camp right on top of the biggest damn tunnel complex in the world. It's a whole city of tunnels. They run for miles. You can drive a vehicle through some of them. Charlie had a hospital, weapons factory, uniform factory-you name it down there. The tunnels go all the way to Cambodia. Charlie kept hitting us and we could never find where he came from or where he went. Found the tunnels by accident. A bulldozer was enlarging the air strip and it fell right through the ground into a tunnel."

"You think..." Boyd still found it hard

to imagine such a configuration so far from any populated area.

"Dunno," Moore conceded. "But it explains things and it also tells us we could be in deep shit here. Sure, those tunnels can hold families. Women and kids. But they can also hide whole battalions of dinks. I ain't feeling too comfortable about this."

"Tell Hardin."

"I did. He didn't pay much attention to me. If we see that kid again, we should try to follow him. But be careful he isn't luring us into an ambush. It's not beyond Charlie to use a kid as a decoy. If they lose one, no sweat. They got lots more. Lots and lots of little dinks."

The night seemed to last a thousand hours. The rain started and stopped several more times, but it made no difference. There was no part of the soldiers that wasn't soaked. Boyd found his skin was extremely itchy. As soon as he satiated the need to scratch one place, another sprang up. The only major break in the monotony was a small disturbance when a common bush snake crawled on The Pope's back and, liking the warmth, decided to stay. Kuhn told him it was a cobra and that he shouldn't move. The Pope remained rigid and in a sweat for several hours before the snake slithered off into the bush. When The Pope saw that it wasn't a cobra, he was in a rage. He came at Kuhn with his knife and was in dead earnest about cutting his throat. Hardin leaped between the two men and just glared The Pope down. He didn't say anything, just stood there until The Pope slowly put his knife away.

"City boys. No sense of humor," Kuhn said, trying to defuse the tension. But everyone knew that what might have been humor several months ago was funny no longer. When The Pope was out of hearing range, Boyd talked to Kuhn about it.

"Just a joke," Kuhn said.

"I know," Boyd agreed, "but things aren't the same. Look at that man's face sometime. Look at mine. He doesn't have eyes anymore, just dark holes in his skull. His expression almost never changes. When a man's eyes change, his mind has changed. He's not the same person. None of us is the same. He wanted to kill you and he will if you do something like that again. No jokes."

"We're friends. We're brothers," Kuhn insisted.

"Yes, but a man who hasn't slept properly in months isn't right in the head. You couldn't see his face because Hardin blocked your view. I saw it. He wanted to kill you, so watch it."

Morning was not much brighter than the night but Hardin knew from his watch it was time to "take da hill." He quietly roused the men and promised them it would not be much further. He didn't know how steep the low mountain was.

They put the sick men near the rear of the column and began the climb. They had little energy at the start, and within two hours they were running on sheer determination. Moore and Boyd each took the point for an hour, then swapped positions. They tried to move quietly but small rocks constantly broke loose and tumbled down the hill. Some of the branches they used for hand-holds cracked and snapped with a sound that would alert a hidden enemy a hundred yards away. Birds were often startled and flew away in a flurry of loud complaints. Hardin fretted about the noisy way they were moving, but there was no easy remedy for it.

There were small monkeys that scolded and often startled them by sudden movements in the trees. They resisted the reflexive impulse to shoot at these unexpected movements. The process strained their nerves and a low murmur of complaining began to reverberate through the jungle.

They were startled by the sound of an air strike no more than two miles away. Then artillery rounds began exploding. The column halted as Hardin tried to get the poop from the command post.

"Aussies ran into bow-cooo shit," he quietly told Jap as he gave the handset back to the radio operator.

"We will, too," Jap said. "You can just feel it. Or smell it."

"Keep 'em moving," Hardin ordered.

They climbed till 1200 hours, rested for twenty minutes, then moved on. They saw absolutely no sign of the enemy.

At 1400 hours Moore came across several spent brass casings from an AK-47. They were new-bright and shiny. At 1430 hours Boyd saw the wire of a simple booby-trap. The wire was connected to a hand grenade that was wedged into the fork of a bush, with the pin pulled. If he had stepped on the wire, the grenade would have popped loose and exploded. But the wire was too visible. The person who built the trap hadn't taken the time to black out the wire with mud or grease. Amateur work, or hasty work? Boyd passed the word, then had a quick conference with Hardin, Jap and Moore.

"I have a feeling someone is working just ahead of us. That looks like it was just set up," Boyd said. The others nodded.

"Move 'bout a quarter click to yo' left. Let's do a little side-shuffle in case dey have set up bigger and better things for us," Hardin ordered.

"What about an air strike up that hill?" Jap suggested.

"No point. We'd be shooting in the dark," Hardin said, dismissing the idea.

The company spent an hour moving across the slope of the mountain before resuming their upward trek. There was no way of knowing if the maneuver confused the Viet Cong but they encountered no further booby traps.

At 1600 hours, Boyd peered over the pinnacle of a flat rock and reported they had reached the top. Ahead of him stretched a flat area, with fewer trees and a tiny bit of visible, dark sky. He studied the area for ten minutes before stepping on to the small plateau, not much bigger than a football field.

Like gray shadows, the men slowly filed over the lip of the ridge and began setting up defensive positions according to Hardin's instructions. Using some C4, they blew down enough trees to allow a Chinook helicopter with a winch to take out their sick comrades. The company commander was half-lucid and insisted he would not be evacuated. Hardin ignored him and within an hour the evacuation was completed. Jap commented that for the first time since he had been in country, the company had no officers at all and maybe now they could do things right. They were quietly pleased with the very large supply of water sent to them in 5-gallon jerry cans.

"They were the lucky ones," Moore said of the evacuees, after drinking a full canteen of water. "At least they got out of this piss hole."

Boyd and Moore tried to dig a foxhole but after digging away three inches of mud, their entrenching tools hit solid rock. They moved a few feet to the right and had no better luck.

"We can't dig through this shit," Moore complained to Jap.

"Keep trying to find a soft spot," was all the advice he could give.

"Oh, I got one-in my head," Moore replied. "For being here."

No one had any better luck, so they abandoned the idea of digging and just scraped a bit of mud into a few sandbags. They would provide minimal protection, but it was something.

Hardin and Jap conducted a survey of their position. Hardin found a tunnel entrance and pointed it out to Jap with the barrel of his rifle. It was under a small ledge, half-hidden by stones and some branches, but the experienced eye would have spotted it easily. Someone had tried to cover it hastily but had done a bad job. Hardin pushed aside the cover material, placed his ear close to the opening and listened. He heard nothing.

The opening was small, slightly larger than the diameter of a basketball, but incredibly it had been cut through solid stone. There was no sign of any excavated material; it had been carefully removed.

"Ever been in a tunnel?" Hardin asked Jap. "Yo' kinda small."

"No, and forget it," Jap answered sharply. "I'll pump in CS, I'll blow them, but I won't go in them. Not for anything."

"Me neither. Tomorrow, we'll try to get some tunnel rats in here," Hardin concluded. "But for now..."

Hardin popped a CS grenade into the

hole and waited, his M-16 ready. They could hear the canister spewing out its heavier-than-air gas that seeped deep into the hole. After twenty minutes they knew that the tunnel was either too big, was blocked further inside, or that no one was in it. They stacked the rocks back over the hole.

When Moore heard about the tunnel entrance, he threw down his entrenching tool and stalked off to find Hardin who was checking if all the trip flares and been place properly.

"We should move outta here-tonight!" he insisted.

"Whatsa big deal?" Hardin asked. "Tunnel's a tunnel. We'll get a Mighty Mite tomorrow and pump in gas. Smoke 'em out, if dey in dere."

"You don't understand. We saw a kid way down at the bottom of the mountain. He kept disappearing, so he must have nipped in and out of tunnels. These tunnels are inter-connected. Do you realize how many V.C. could be in there? When they have their families with them, you can bet the farm it's a big unit."

"How many?" Hardin challenged the assertion. "How far yo' think a tunnel goes?"

"How far?" Moore threw the question

back. "To the North Pole if they want. These dinks can dig through anything. They have been digging these tunnels since the French were here. I've seen some of them. Look, we're an under-strength company. How many men we got? Less than a hundred? Just report that we found some tunnels and we should be lifted the fuck outta here."

"Our orders are to set up a base of operations here," Hardin insisted, pointing his finger at the ground. "We're supposed to find these tunnels and search 'em. We found 'em. We stay till the job's done."

Word spread quickly about the tunnel and about Moore's fears. There was considerable talk and consternation. Jap found merit in Moore's argument.

"I think he's right," Jap said to Hardin as they ate some C-rations. "Listen to him. The 25th had a lot of experience with tunnels."

"So?" Hardin replied. "Whatsa big deal? If Charlie's hiding in tunnels, we'll flush his ass out."

"We have no idea how many entrances there are. We don't know how many dinks are in there," Jap reminded him.

"So?" Hardin persisted, licking the back of his plastic spoon and wiping the back of his hand across his mouth. "We never know. Same-o, same-o. Right?"

"Well, I gotta bad feeling about this," Jap said, abandoning the argument. He knew that when Hardin dug in his heels over something, nothing would move. "The other men do, too. They're counting on you to do the right thing. He who runs away..."

"Yeah, lives to fight another day. Well, I gotta bad feeling," Hardin said, rubbing his stomach. "Goddam C-rats will kill me before Charlie ever does. Dis is some goddam rock pile we sitting on. Can't even dig a hole to bury cans or shit in."

The platoon sergeants spread the word that they wanted maximum alertness. Only one man in three was to sleep at a time, for no more than two hours. They put out every Claymore they had and cleaned their weapons rigorously. Listening posts were put out only fifty yards down the slope. They were to come into the perimeter at the first sign of trouble.

Hardin and Jap plotted some artillery concentrations in front of their positions and radioed them to the New Zealand artillery battery. Jap seemed extremely tense and on edge. He couldn't seem to stand still, but kept shifting his weight from foot to foot and fiddling with the safety on his rifle. Hardin noticed the performance.

"I swear, yo' becoming a little ol' granny," Hardin said, glaring down at the smaller man.

"I'd like to live long enough to be one!" Jap snapped back, and went off to check his men.

The order against sleeping was unnecessary, for no one had any intention of doing so. They stayed wide awake, without any talking or whispering. The rain settled into a steady downpour, the sounds providing a mask for anyone who might be moving about. Boyd's eyes seemed to play a dozen tricks on him. He made a point of not focusing on one spot too long because when he did the shadows moved ominously. The blackness seemed to slide into the gray area, first producing inky clouds as if an octopus was suspended in the jungle. Then they took on human forms, gliding and blowing about. He closed his eyes, rubbed the lids vigorously, then looked again. The forms were gone.

Moore lay beside him, his M-16 resting on a sandbag. The man seemed to have an endless supply of chiclets, their peppermint smell permeating the air. Boyd wondered if the Viet Cong could smell them. After three hours of listening to the man snap and chew, Boyd finally whispered to him to give it a break.

As was always the case, time stood still. Every time Boyd checked the luminous hands of his watch, they seemed not to have moved at all. He tried to pass the time by thinking pleasant thoughts. He ran out of ideas in minutes. His mind kept going back to Knowles, and the moments before they put him on the helicopter. Boyd couldn't forget that face, that beaming smile of a man with a shattered leg, a man who thought he would soon be snatched from hell. He touched the little statue in his pocket and wondered if Knowles had kept it, if he would have had good luck instead of bad. He thought about Olive Oyl and tried to picture a bowling alley in Saigon. Where had he put it? He wondered something else, too. If the war ever ended, what would become of Olive Oyl? It's one thing to go over the hill in the U.S., but what becomes of a man who is AWOL in Vietnam when the troops go home? Does he just try to jump aboard a plane and go with them? At some point in time, he would have to pay the piper and it might mean a long prison sentence. But Olive Oyl always had a plan. He was a human cat. No matter how the army dropped him, he always landed on his feet.

His mind turned inward and he contemplated his own future. His resume would be most impressive. No job. No skills. No education. Great beginning. Combat skills had little translation in civilian life. Maybe police work. He knew he could get money to go back to school, but he hated school. He shook the gloom from his head and stared again at the blackness. Again, he saw something move. Close to the ground.

He blinked, turned his head away a moment, then looked back. It wasn't moving but it was there. A form. A lump. Something. He nudged Moore, who grunted softly. His arm felt rigid and Boyd sensed him raising the stock of his rifle. He had seen it, too.

The thing was forty feet away, near the ground, and it was sliding towards them. He didn't want to set off a false alarm but he wasn't going to wait forever, either.

They had been watching a man, who rose slowly to a crouched position. Moore squeezed off a textbook "burst of three" that knocked the guerrilla backwards.

"Sappers!" was the only word Moore shouted, then swung his rifle to the right and cut down another dark form that had suddenly appeared out of the blackness.

The jungle suddenly erupted with noise and brilliant flashes that danced about like huge fireflies. Tracers burned over their heads. The roar of American weapons and exploding Claymores answered back. The Viet Cong and Americans were firing at each other at almost point-blank range-AK-47's against M-16's. Chicom machine guns against their M-60's.

Men were hit immediately on both sides. Voices mixed with the thunder of guns. It was an unintelligible babel of curses, cries of pain and terror. Boyd emptied one magazine along his assigned "final protection line" and grabbed another magazine he had laid on the sandbag, a plastic bag over it for protection from the rain.

He seemed all thumbs and couldn't get it into its slot. Moore emptied his magazine, too. For several fateful seconds, neither one of them was firing. Boyd glanced up and saw the vague outline of men running towards them. One fell, struck by someone else's bullet. One ran right past them, either not seeing them or having some other specific destination. A third fired a burst from his AK that struck Moore in the arm and side. Boyd heard the bullets hit and Moore groan.

Boyd abandoned the effort to load his rifle and leaped to his feet. He charged like a bull at the guerrilla who had temporarily swung his rifle to shoot towards The Pope. He probably never saw the American coming.

Boyd screamed and hit the man so hard with the butt of his M-16 that the plastic stock shattered. The Viet Cong flew backwards and hit the ground like a broken puppet. Boyd grabbed the AK-47 and shot two Viet Cong running past him, intent upon breaking through the perimeter. In the darkness, everything was becoming mixed up and chaotic.

Bullets whipped past Boyd's head and he realized that anyone standing up was a potential target for everyone, including his own men. He threw himself to the ground, rolled to one side and began scuttling like a crab back to his position. He hadn't intended to scream when he hit the guerrilla. The sound had just uncontrollably leaped from his lungs. It was what the drill instructor had tried to get him to do in bayonet practice but he never could. But this wasn't a man sticking points into a dummy. This was an animal fighting for survival.

Powerful explosions rocked the ground

and illuminated the sky. Hardin had called for the artillery battery to fire the def-cons he had plotted. The explosions were so close Boyd heard the shrapnel flying over his head.

In the darkness he ended up in The Pope's position, rather than his own. The Pope fired a burst that went wide but tore off part of Boyd's ear.

"It's Boyd!" he pleaded as he crawled towards the sandbags.

The Pope swung his muzzle to the right and Boyd rolled over the low barricade and landed on something lumpy and hard.

"We're getting overrun!" The Pope shouted. "We gotta pull back."

"Yeah! Where's Kuhn?" Boyd asked.

"You're on top of him. He bought it," The Pope shouted. "Crawl back. I'll cover you, then you cover me!"

Boyd needed no further urging. Despite heavy losses, the Viet Cong showed no sign of letting up their attack. They had moved hundreds of men through the network of tunnels that stretched for miles to jumping off positions all around the Americans. The carefully-concealed entrances had been opened and the coordinated attack began exactly on cue. They had canvas bags of explosives, hand grenades and

RPG2 rockets.

Boyd slid back a dozen yards, then turned and fired the AK at a man kneeling with an RPG2 on his shoulder. The guerrilla fired the rocket just as the bullet hit him, the projectile soaring wildly into the air before bursting high up in the trees.

"Pope! C'mon!" he shouted. There was no answer and no movement.

"Pope!" he shouted once more, then rolled to his right just before a long burst of machine gun fire splattered off the rocks where he had been lying.

He was disoriented as to where he was but Jap had heard his voice.

"Over here!" the sergeant called out as he squeezed off two short bursts with his M-16.

Boyd needed no further encouragement. He scrambled on his hands and knees another ten yards and lay down next to Jap behind a puny line of sandbags.

"Watch behind us," Jap warned. "They're in the perimeter. Anyone moves, kill him."

"Haven't got my rifle," Boyd reported. "Just got an AK."

"Take mine," Jap said. "I'm hit in the chest. Having trouble firing it, anyway."

"Where's Wop?" Boyd asked.

"Pinned down like everyone else," Jap answered as he lobbed a grenade with his left hand. It was a limp "girl's" throw but his target was only thirty yards away. The grenade exploded, ripping into a two-man Viet Cong machine gun team that was trying to set up a heavy weapon.

They heard Hardin's voice shouting on the radio but had no idea what he was saying. His words were garbled by gunfire and explosions. Had they been able to hear, they would have known he was talking to a FAC. And if they had the special privilege of circling above the battlefield in a small plane, they would have know that American fire power was arriving from several bases. A cargo plane began making lazy loops over the mountain, its crew throwing out boxes of flares suspended from small parachutes. Cobras circled just beyond, waiting like hungry beasts for a feast. F-4's from Bien Hoa were high above them, asking for their share of the targets.

This firepower would be of little use if the Americans couldn't keep a safety gap between themselves and Viet Cong. The guerrillas knew it. They employed their tactic they had learned so well: "Grab the enemy by the belt and hold on to him."

The sky and ground took on a brilliant, red glow as the flares lit up the ground below. The two adversaries could now see each other well, and this only added to the ferocity of their death struggle.

Hardin knew what had to be done. The Viet Cong had to be thrown back down the slope far enough for air power to destroy them. He told his radio operator to stay on the air no matter what, then gathered five men from nearby positions. He stood and roared out in a bull voice what he wanted.

"Drive 'em back! Push 'em down the hill!"

Fewer than half the company was able to answer. Hesitant at first, but then with a peculiar frenzy that spelled "it's this or die," they counter-attacked. They fired whole magazines in two short bursts, threw what grenades they had left, then reloaded and seized another ten yards of ground. A quarter of the survivors went down in these crucial seconds. The brilliant lights of the flares made the entire area seem like a baseball stadium with a game being played under the lights. Everyone could now see everyone and the battle disintegrated into dozens of small fights, clusters of men shooting and hacking away at their opponents. The hill top looked like an area filled with gladiators.

Hardin wasn't running. He was moving in a slow walk, firing steadily and shouting encouragement to the others. Boyd rose to join him. Jap struggled to his knees but no further. He was bleeding profusely and had no weapon, anyway. Boyd saw Moore swing his entrenching tool with his good hand into a Viet Cong's face. He tried to fight his way towards his friend, but found his way suddenly blocked by a guerrilla who lunged at him with the bayonet on his AK-47. It was a clumsy attempt that Boyd easily side-stepped, then shattered the side of the man's skull with his AK. But when he turned back, Moore had disappeared.

The Viet Cong vigilantly tried to stand their ground, but the sheer ferocity of the fire power they faced was more than any soldiers, no matter how dedicated, could withstand. They began falling back, at first a few feet at a time, in short leaps, then running pell-mell away from the machine that was tearing them up. Their senior commander was dismayed and had enough experience to know what was at stake. If American air power could be brought into play, the battle would be lost.

He screamed, cursed and kicked his men back up the slope. His subordinate commanders got the last of their units out of the tunnels and into a loose skirmish line. He knew the American force was depleted-on its last legs. One more push could do it. The Americans seemed to be collected around a giant of a man, a black man, who stood like a rock, oblivious to the firestorm around him. He was their standard, their flag, and they rallied to him. Without him, the others would be broken and scattered like dried twigs. The guerrilla leader dispatched his best marksman to a position just below an outgrowth of rock. It was not a difficult shot.

The sniper decided against a head shot. The target was moving too much. He concentrated on the torso.

Hardin fell sideways when the first bullet struck him in the left side. It was a grazing wound and the bullet followed along the rib line and exited through his back. It felt like a heavyweight boxer's punch and momentarily took the wind out of him. Boyd fired the last bullets in his rifle, making the sniper dive for cover, then tried to pull Hardin behind another man's body for crude protection. It wasn't necessary because Hardin got up again.

"Where dat bastard?" he gasped.

"By those rocks, I think," Boyd answered, pointing to their right.

Hardin rose into a crouch, like a runner about to start a race, then sprang forward and ran straight towards the man's position. The Viet Cong came up over the top of the rock pile, rifle ready for another shot. He expected his target to be fifty feet away. He pulled back impulsively because the giant was nearly on top of him. Without aiming, he fired again. He couldn't possibly have missed.

The bullet went straight into Hardin's stomach and out the back, missing the spinal cord but making an exit hole the size of a man's fist. The American stumbled momentarily, then came on, running.

The sniper dropped his rifle and tried to run but Hardin let out a roar and made a flying tackle that sent both of them crashing down the slope. Hardin was on his feet so quickly, it seemed that he wasn't wounded at all. He smashed the sniper's head so hard against a rock that he could hear the skull shatter. In a flash, he shoved his Buck knife under the man's chin and into the brain.

Another Viet Cong shot him from close range, two bullets hitting his arm and shoulder. Hardin stabbed him under the rib cage, wrenching the AK away at the same time. He emptied it into two Viet Cong who had just pulled themselves up the slope to where they could see the battle. Hardin killed one, then threw the empty weapon at the other man, who quickly retreated. Suddenly alone, Hardin walked back up the hill, part way across the top, and slowly knelt down. Boyd knelt beside him and fired a burst from an M-16 he had picked up. Hardin put one hand on Boyd's shoulder to steady himself.

"Doan let 'em...overrun...us," he said to Boyd, then closed his eyes. He remained kneeling but Boyd felt the strength slowly go out of his hand.

The Viet Cong made their final push but the Americans gave back not one inch of ground. Men shot at each other from a distance of inches, not feet. Knives, entrenching tools and machetes were used as commonly as guns.

The guerrillas had a numerical edge of five to one and had regained their lost momentum. This was not lost upon Hardin's radio operator who put into effect the "final order" Hardin had given him. He told the FAC to "paste everything," then tried to find some shelter under a dead man's body.

The Cobras pounced first, flying two abreast, firing rockets and 20-mm shells that smashed into the rocks and trees, sending metal fragments into wood, earth and flesh. They fell in piles and rows, American and Vietnamese mixed together. Those who survived the first attack desperately sought cover of any kind. The Cobras made their second pass and all effective fighting ended. Men who had been standing toe to toe in deadly battle ran together and squeezed into rock crevices and under outcrops, huddling in the scant hope of not being blown to bits. Some Viet Cong were fortunate enough to get back into their tunnels, but most could not find the entrances in all the confusion.

The F-4's attacked singly, dropping cluster bomb units that walked up the slope and across the top of the mountain. A second flight added 250-pound bombs. The huge explosions shook the ground so hard that some of the smaller tunnels caved in.

Miles away, they artillery gunners sweated and strained as they went through the endless rhythm of ramming shells into the breaches, pulling the lanyards, ejecting the spent brass, then repeating the cycle. The pile of spent shell casing behind each gun grew higher than a man. The barrels grew red hot and some would soon wear out.

The artillery bombardment went on most of the night and each flight of aircraft was replaced by another as soon as its payload was spent. The flare ship stayed on station the entire night, dropping more than 2,000 flares in all. At 0600 the Australian brigadier ordered the fire lifted and boldly inserted a platoon of his troops right on to the mountain top, the helicopters hovering a few feet above the smashed landscape, tense crews wondering if they would be raked by heavy weapons.

The Aussies quickly moved to the edge of the slope and set up their security. It was very difficult to see anything, as the air was filled with a dense "London fog" of smoke and debris. As experienced as they were, the battle scene nearly shocked them like nothing they had ever witnessed. They groped and peered among the carnage for half an hour before finding the first American survivor. The radio operator was still breathing despite dozens of wounds from the CBU's. Another man was alive, despite the loss of his left arm. He had been partially protected by three bodies that had fallen over him. Two Viet Cong were rousted from under a rock ledge, bleeding from the ears. A bomb blast had broken their ear drums and they were unable to stand. They babbled incoherently and trembled when anyone came near them. For some unknown reason, they had taken off their clothes.

When they saw Hardin's body, it was clear where the final fight had taken place. Piles of American and Vietnamese bodies were scattered about his, prompting one hardened veteran to shake his head in dismay and say something about "Custer's Last Stand."

They found Wop's body leaning against a pile of blasted rock rubble, both legs gone below the knees, morphine needles sticking out of his thighs like a porcupine. The way he was positioned, it looked as if he had propped himself up to watch the battle as he killed himself with drugs before he bled to death.

"Guess you didn't suffer too much, then, did you mate?" a soldier said sadly as he looked at the almost happy expression on the medic's face.

An hour later, the brigadier flew in to make a personal inspection tour. He stood in the center of it all, his staff gathered around him in stunned silence. He didn't speak for ten minutes, then shook his head and gave the order to evacuate the dead.

"A victory, gentlemen. We have an incredible victory here," he said in a cracked voice, then looked around as if defying anyone to dispute his conclusion. Then he flew back to his headquarters to organize the follow-up and to prepare the action report. His staff estimated that 600 Viet Cong had died in the fighting. Many more were probably wounded and hiding in the tunnels. They would spend four days trying to flush them out, but would catch very few of them. Aided by their families, the guerrillas melted away through the dozens of entrances that were miles from the battle scene.

The Australians took the bodies away using nets slung below Chinook helicopters. A three-star general flew down from MACV in Saigon and made notes for the next day's briefing while an army photographer shot five rolls of film for the military history branch. The general increased the number of Viet Cong dead to 950. In a war of "body counts" it was important to maintain a ten-to-one kill ratio. Ninety-six American soldiers had died. It was a matter of arithmetic. Simple arithmetic.

Edith Boyd sat silently on the edge of a high-back chair as the young National Guard lieutenant removed the contents of a cardboard box. She had thought about dusting and vacuuming the room before his arrival, but had decided it didn't matter.

"I was the escort officer for your son," he said. "He was buried at Arlington. He received full military honors."

He gave her the folded flag from her son's coffin, four medals in leather cases, a death certificate, a letter from Robert's battalion commander extolling his courage and dedication, a letter from the battalion chaplain urging her to be brave. It ended with a Biblical passage. He gave her a letter from the Secretary of Defense expressing his appreciation and regrets.

"He didn't have much in the way of personal effects," the officer said. "Just these small items."

He handed her a tiny ivory statue of Buddha, a crude drawing of a skull with a caption called the "Ninth Infantry Division Prayer," a page torn from a book of poetry, and a diary, wrapped in plastic that was soiled with smeary red clay. It had a stale odor of death about it.

"You're the beneficiary of his life insurance," the officer went on to say.

"Oh? How much is that?" she asked.

"Ten thousand dollars," the lieutenant replied. "The standard G.I. policy."

"Seems fair," she said. "Ten thousand dollars for a son. If I had ten sons, and they were all killed, I would be rich. I really must thank the President for having this war."

"Mrs. Boyd..."

"Sorry. I'm not blaming you," she said, waving her hand as if to dismiss her own rudeness. "Have you ever been in Vietnam?"

"No," he answered frankly.

"I noticed you don't have any of those..." she hesitated for lack of the word, pointing at his uniform.

"Ribbons," he assisted her. "No, I don't have any battle ribbons. I'm just in the Guard. But we do try to help the families."

He was obviously uncomfortable and wanted to be on his way. He hated the job of escort officer and wondered why his C.O. kept sticking him with it. This was the third time he had performed the duty and the strain was terrible. Families said they didn't blame him, but they did. He represented what they were angry about, and no matter what they said, he felt the fury and frustration.

"I didn't go to Arlington," she continued. "I didn't think it really mattered. Robert and I weren't very close. After his father left me, he became very...difficult. A breach opened up between us and I could never close it."

"I'm sorry," the lieutenant said, casting a wishful eye towards the door.

"He volunteered for Vietnam. Did you know that?"

"No, I didn't," he replied. "I haven't read his record."

"He wanted to spite me. He wanted to hurt me. He was my only child. So, he did a good job of it."

"I'm sorry," he said again. He was starting to sound like a stuck record.

"If you love one thing, and you lose that one thing, then you lose it all, don't you?" she asked.

"I guess so," he replied. "I've never had that happen to me. I can't feel what you're feeling."

"No," she agreed. "You can't."

He left her sitting in the chair, staring at nothing, the letters and book on her lap. He felt like a man freed from a tomb and vowed he'd never do another escort assignment if he had to go to jail for insubordination.

After twenty minutes, Edith Boyd carefully removed the plastic and fingered the bent, dirty blue cover of the diary. She read the first entry, then turned to the last.

Day 247. Rumor is we're going out soon. Somewhere down south. Getting to be old hat. I had a funny thought this morning. In all the time I've been here, all the places I've been, I never saw a flower. What kind of country is that? Olive Oyl is the smart one. He always was. I got bad vibes about this operation. I wish Olive Oyl was here to say, "Don't look good, brothers. Don't look good at all." Vietnam slowly eats away a man's insides until he doesn't feel any more. He talks, he walks around, he gets drunk. But he doesn't really feel. It's a cancer that eats the soul and devours the heart. The Pope no longer believes in God. Wop no longer believes in medicine. Hardin doesn't believe in the army, and I no longer believe in anything. I'm tired. So very, very tired. I think I want to go home.

About The Author

Steven N. Spetz was born in Pittsburgh, Pennsylvania and graduated from the University of Pittsburgh in 1962. He was first in his R.O.T.C. (Reserve Officer Training Corps) class and was commissioned a second lieutenant in the Regular Army-Artillery. He served in Italy and Germany from 1962-1966, then in Vietnam with the 9th Infantry Division as the fire support officer of an infantry battalion. In 1968 he resigned his commission as a captain and emigrated to Canada where he pursued his writing career while teaching social studies. He and his wife, Glenda, have co-authored twenty-three books, including three previous novels.

WATCH FOR THESE NEW COMMONWEALTH BOOKS

WATCH FOR THESE NEW COMMONWEALTH BOOKS

	ISBN #	U.S.	Can
❏ **RIBBONS AND ROSES**, D.B. Taylor	1-55197-088-0	$4.99	$6.99
❏ **PRISON DREAMS**, John O. Powers	1-55197-039-2	$4.99	$6.99
❏ **A VOW OF CHASTITY,** Marcia Jean Greenshields	1-55197-106-2	$4.99	$6.99
❏ **LAVENDER'S BLUE**, Janet Tyers	1-55197-058-9	$4.99	$6.99
❏ **HINTS AND ALLEGATIONS,** Kimberly A. Dascenzo	1-55197-073-2	$4.99	$6.99
❏ **BROKEN BRIDGES**, Elizabeth Gorlay	1-55197-119-4	$4.99	$6.99
❏ **PAINTING THE WHITE HOUSE,** Hal Marcovitz	1-55197-095-3	$4.99	$6.99
❏ **THE KISS OF JUDAS**, J.R. Thompson	1-55197-045-7	$4.99	$6.99
❏ **BALLARD'S WAR**, Tom Holzel	1-55197-112-7	$4.99	$6.99
❏ **ROSES FOR SARAH**, Anne Philips	1-55197-125-9	$4.99	$6.99
❏ **THE TASKMASTER**, Mary F. Murchison	1-55197-113-5	$4.99	$6.99
❏ **SECOND TIME**, Thomas E. Sprain	1-55197-135-6	$4.99	$6.99
❏ **MY BROTHER'S TOWN**, B.A. Stuart	1-55197-138-0	$4.99	$6.99
❏ **MISSING PIECES**, Carole W. Holden	1-55197-172-0	$4.99	$6.99
❏ **DIARY OF A GHOST,** Alice Richards Laule	1-55197-132-1	$4.99	$6.99

Available at your local bookstore or use this page to order.

Send to: COMMONWEALTH PUBLICATIONS INC.
9764 - 45th Avenue
Edmonton, Alberta, CANADA T6E 5C5

Please send me the items I have checked above. I am enclosing
$_____ (please add $2.50 per book to cover postage and
handling). Send check or money order, no cash or C.O.D.'s, please.

Mr./Mrs./Ms._____

Address_____

City/State_____ Zip_____

Please allow four to six weeks for delivery.
Prices and availability subject to change without notice.

When Private Robert Boyd impulsively purchased and began keeping a personal diary, Vietnam was just a name. It is through his diary entries that the reader experiences Boyd's rites of passage from a "Cherry" (new arrival in Vietnam) to a hardened and disillusioned combat veteran who is transformed from adolescence to old age in a matter of months.

Vietnam Diary brings home the horror and trauma of war in the jungle and rice paddies where there is only one law—survival—and where each hour is an entire lifetime.

Vietnam Diary

by
Steven Spetz

Available at your local bookstore or use this page to order.

❏ 1-55197-133-X – VIETNAM DIARY –
   $4.99 U.S./$6.99 in Canada
Send to: COMMONWEALTH PUBLICATIONS INC.
   9764 - 45th Avenue
   Edmonton, Alberta, CANADA T6E 5C5

Please send me the items I have checked above. I am enclosing $_____ (please add $2.50 per book to cover postage and handling). Send check or money order, no cash or C.O.D.'s, please.

Mr./Mrs./Ms._____

Address_____

City/State_____ Zip_____

Please allow four to six weeks for delivery.
Prices and availability subject to change without notice.